SECRETS TO PARENTING WITHOUT GIVING A F^CK

The Non-Conformist Playbook to Raising Happy Kids Without Public Meltdowns, Power Struggles, & Punishments

SUE DONNELLAN

Library of Congress Cataloging-in-Publication Data is available.

ISBN: 978-0-578-84383-4

Illustration: Colleen Davis, www.IntentionalBranding.com
Author Photo: Ampersand Studios, Boise ID
Indexer: Meridith Murray

Ask Mom Publishing, LLC.

TABLE OF CONTENTS

In Loving Gratitude To:

My spectacular husband Tim,
My inspirational children:
Matt, Kelly, Scott, & Derek
&
My cherished parents

Acknowledgements

Three years ago, in the midst of chasing my tail with four teenagers, creativity specialist Sandra Cavanaugh began helping me pull this book out from the depths of my soul. The words *thank you* will never be enough. Your brilliance, intuitiveness, and pure love shine through every word. You empowered me to put my life's purpose on paper and I'll forever be grateful.

There are many talented people who took a chance on a new writer by deciding to work with me anyway. This book would not have become all I envisioned and hoped it would be without these gifted professionals: Katie McCoach, Michelle Kulp, Lisa Florenzen, Colleen Davis, Janice Harper, and Rachel VanDyken. Special thank you to all my clients, the frustrated parents who allowed me to guide them through stressful, chaotic times, emerging triumphant on the other side of their parenting overwhelm.

Last, but never least, my family who lovingly taught me the life lessons I needed to learn so I could share them with the world and help others. Your honesty has been my greatest gift.

Foreword

We are all products of our upbringing and the belief systems that have been embedded in us from our own parents and society. Even though most of us have the best intentions when parenting our kids, we still get to the point where we've run out of our own ideas to solve a problem and we'd just like to know what else to do.

Secrets to Parenting Without Giving a F^ck prepared me for how to handle my kids' challenging behavior before it even happens. Sue Donnellan provides an amazing resource to tap into when you're feeling that you need advice from *that friend*, whose opinion and advice you trust the most.

Taking time to pause and read Sue's invaluable tried and true systems will save you not only time but the heartache, stress, and the frustration of feeling helpless and ineffective with your own children. (It works for husbands too!)

Sue's unique perspective gives us a plethora of new ideas, with a no BS approach that is *results* oriented. Each section had more golden nuggets than the last and the more I read the more hooked I became. Who doesn't want results!?

Some of the most essential topics of parenting are tackled: eliminating yelling and guilt, being a role model, shedding parenting patterns that aren't working, and empowering your children and yourself to make decisions quickly and effectively. Sue helped me to find a way to organize my thoughts so I could get my life and household set up like a well-oiled machine. This more harmonious environment has helped my family thrive because when mommy is happy, life is a lot easier for all of us! Everyone in my life will forever thank Sue for introducing me to these methods.

Practical strategies are laid out in a step-by-step manner through personal stories and self-reflective insights. I learned that one of the most effective ways to influence our kids is by always setting an example as their role model and Sue shows you just how to do that. By learning the right mix of guidance and letting go, we create a fun, functional, and inspiring environment for our kids. The irony is, it's because we actually do give a f^ck!

I'm excited to introduce this book to you because it affirms the results my husband and I achieved by doing our best and being open to learning and evolving, as well as the values my parents showed me – unconditional love and mutual respect. I learned endless valuable lessons from my parents. I learned what to do, along with a bit of what not to do (even though I feel bad saying that because my mom will read this.) Relax, Mom. The "What not to do's" were mostly from Dad!

The guiding principles of parenting that my husband and I believe in are to raise kids we like, to help them embrace their unique talents, and to teach them to show respect and kindness for others. Lastly, it's so important to have fun and not take things too seriously. In that same spirit, *Secrets to Parenting Without Giving a F^ck* delivers the playbook to parenting our kids into adulthood. The foundation my husband and I are creating has been enhanced tenfold after being connected with Sue, and for that we will be eternally grateful.

Lana Gomez Maniscalco, Artist, Wife, Mom of two, Creative Director, *What's Wrong With People, Inc.*

How Did I Get Here?

"I'm Never Having Kids."

How does someone who never wanted kids end up writing a parenting book?

During my youth, and I'm talking from 5 – 25 years old, the thought of being someone's mother was…unthinkable! My friends wouldn't have described me as warm and fuzzy around kids, either. I wasn't the sort of person you'd see bending down and coochie-cooing with babies or asking to hold a newborn.

In fact, most of my friends knew not to trust me around kids. Take, for example, while on a date at Pizza Hut in my teens, I stuck my foot out and tripped some ankle biters whose parents let them run rampant around the restaurant. I felt as though I needed to do my small part to teach those kids what their parents hadn't. Stay in your seat and be respectful while dining. No one wants hear, see, or trip over out of control kids.

Even when I babysat, I moved the clocks ahead and convinced the little ones I let them stay up late. "Hurry! Get to sleep so your parents don't find out I let you stay awake past bedtime." Once safely tucked into their beds, my boyfriend's feet hit the pedals of his bike, making haste to the house. Yes, I was every parent's nightmare.

Born the youngest in a family with an older brother, I had no experience with kids and didn't want any! Watching parents struggle to corral their kids, begging them to behave, then going to bed in sheer exhaustion to get up and do it all again, seemed utterly thankless and mundane to me. There appeared to be no other way for parenting to exist in anyone's life, other than to have children be the center of their universe. Even back then, I had an understanding that kids should not be our full identity or a direct reflection of who we are. They are their own people. Plus, I never wanted to be that needed.

Along with being anti-kid, marriage wasn't much of a draw either. Marriage looked like a prison sentence as I watched miserable couples come through my cashier line during my late teenage retail days. They argued over how much money was spent, or the husband flirted openly in front of his wife. She wore her wedding ring, he didn't. Who needed any part of that nonsense? Certainly not me. Besides, how could someone possibly be happy with the same person forever? Love? What is love, anyway? I'm good on my own. I've got this.

Given my attitudes about marriage and kids, I spent my youth loving my freedom and selfish years. You'd find me at the table having my cake and eating it, too!

"Who's He?"

College years were a continuation of being free spirited. So happily free, I routinely chastised my college roommate for being engaged so young. She could have wallpapered her room with Polaroids (it was the 80's) of me making gag gestures while holding up her *Bride* magazines.

I suppose it turned out to be fitting, then, that me and that same engaged roommate were sitting together in the Sweet Shoppe at Purdue, when something caused me to glance up from my book. There, from across the room, a vision of hotness in jeans and a t-shirt caught my eye. "Deb, there's my husband," I blurted without thinking, as my jaw hung open. Somehow, upon laying eyes on this guy, my plan of "no marriage, never kids" suddenly self-destructed on the spot. They say a "soulmate is a stranger you recognize" and I recognized him immediately.

With graduation four short months away, I absolutely needed to connect with this stranger. But how could I do that, when my old school sense of etiquette didn't enable me to ask a guy out? I did what any woman who didn't want her future potential husband to slip through her hands would do. I sent my best guy friend John over to tell him to ask me out.

Tim. I loved his name the first time I heard it. On our first date, he took me flying. He had his civilian pilot's license, which he hoped to use to become an Air Force Fighter Pilot. We dated for my last four months of college and kept a casual long-distance relationship after graduation. I went back to NYC as he finished his engineering degree before he headed to pilot training.

While Tim had massive potential as a future husband, I wasn't quite ready to act on it. We kept our relationship low-pressure. I started my career in advertising sales for a trade magazine, got my graduate degree at night, and traveled with friends to quaint European cities. I dated a few other guys, but still made time to see Tim whenever we could be in the same city. There's also a lot to be said for the art of old-fashioned letter writing in long-distance relationships. Real letter writing. Notebook paper, pen, envelope, and a stamp. We both still have all our letters from those days.

While Tim was training, I enjoyed my advertising sales job and began to form fun friendships with my co-workers. During a memorable lunch together, a colleague mentioned the "crazy-real" experience he had with a tea leaf reader over the weekend. He challenged all of us to visit so we could compare notes during our next lunch.

A charming, grandmotherly type, this woman informed me of her alleged magical intuitive abilities while I sipped fresh-brewed hot tea. Once consumed, she peered into my cup and predicted my future simply by "studying" the remnants of the leaves left behind. I immediately knew she was full of crap when she confidently made her first prediction. "I see you with four children!"

Me, a mom of four? Quack. I had just wasted forty dollars and thirty minutes of my time. At least the tea tasted good. The tea leaf lady also saw me marrying a man in uniform whose name began with the letter "T," along with some other spicy tidbits. I wrote this experience off as just good fun because I didn't believe her never-going-to-happen predictions. Although I did have a guy in my life whose name started with a "T," and yes, people who fly in the military wear dress whites, or is it blues? Still, they wear a uniform. Coincidence. That's all.

By the time I was twenty-four, three years after we met, Tim and I grew more serious and decided to date exclusively long-distance. Over time, I watched while he passionately chased his dreams. I marveled at the consistency of his words and his actions. I met his amazing family and I blissfully laughed my ass off whenever we were together. I realized I lucked out meeting a man who made marriage seem like it wouldn't suck. It's often been asked of people in love, "How do you know?"

What I discovered? When you absolutely can't imagine life without that person, it's for real.

Tim was the most self-confident and altruistic guy I'd ever met. I found him to be exceptionally loyal, smart, handsome, and 100% my equal. Soon enough, I realized he had become the love of my life.

As it happened, he also loved children. While we dated, I tried warning him I didn't like kids. He didn't quite believe me and asked me to marry him anyway.

I turned twenty-seven when we married. By then I had quit my advertising sales job to start my own sales business, while Tim had just begun his military career flying fighter jets in Valdosta, Georgia. Being married and kid-free turned out to be quite fun. I look back with nostalgia at being able to nap whenever we were tired, eat at our favorite restaurants, vacation at will, and basically just be us and our two German shepherds.

"Knock. Knock. I'm Ready."

After four years of marriage, we were both fulfilled in our jobs. Over those four years, I witnessed firsthand how my husband adored friends' babies and how tenderly he took care of our two German shepherds. Maybe I could consider having a baby for this amazing man. He never pressured me. But these eggs weren't getting any fresher… and how bad could it really be?

Believe me, though, I made sure he was aware that having his baby was the nicest thing I could ever do for him.

I knew our first baby would be a boy because of a recurring dream where a three-month-old boy visited me. I held him in my arms as we looked out the bedroom window. We were surrounded by bright, airy light and we both felt at peace. I knew he was waiting for me to be ready to bring him into my life. It felt as though forces greater than myself were at play, gently nudging me toward motherhood in my sleep. I didn't share that with Tim, as he might think the soon-to-be mother of his child was nuts. Matthew was born in March, 1998.

"Are You F^cking Kidding Me?"

Two and a half years later and knee deep in the terrible twos, Tim and I were permanently bent over backward, trying to accommodate this one demanding child. He threw food off his highchair and he mocked us by dropping his pacifier and having us pick up his toys. Tim and I tripped over each other to see who could satisfy his needs first. During one particular breakfast outing at Cracker Barrel with Matt in his highchair, Tim and I almost smacked heads trying to be the first to pick up his dropped muffin. I looked across the table at my husband and said, "It's time to try for our second baby. Matt needs someone else in his life to focus on besides us."

Kicking my Type A personality into high gear, I read a fertility book to master my ovulation "timing" so we could have a girl with certainty. I had no plans to get pregnant a third time, and I knew I wouldn't change my mind. I laid out the schedule for Tim to follow, and like a man he made the deal go down as needed. Strategic, under control, we scheduled our baby-making, specifically, girl-making.

Soon, the stick read "pregnant." I experienced basic morning sickness and a feeling of blah for the first three months, but in general things were uneventful and I felt thankful. Close to the four-month point however, a slight complication triggered an immediate ultrasound. I was considered low-risk, and, honestly, I wasn't worried. Tim never missed an appointment, but he had to miss this one. He was scheduled for mandatory time in the air traffic tower on the military base.

As I lay on the ultrasound table, the words that changed my life forever came out of the technician's mouth.

Technician: "Were you on fertility?"

Me: "No, why?"

Technician: "There are three babies in there!"

Those words hung in the air like the scent of three stinky diapers. "Are you f^cking kidding me?!" I inhaled and I don't think I've exhaled since. In an instant, my mind flashed to how drastically my life would change. A bigger car, a bigger house, never-ending amounts of food, four college tuitions! How could I go from one to four kids this quickly when I never wanted ANY children?? Triplets?! Not to mention the idea of my poor body stretching to the size of Texas.

I made myself three promises:

1. I will not give up my business I worked so hard to build.
2. I will not sell the little sports car I bought during my single days.
3. No matter how many kids I have, I will not drive a minivan!

Hearing the tech's words shocked me so violently, I needed her to get my phone from my purse so I could call Tim. Hands shaking, mind racing, I barely remembered his phone number. With him being in the air traffic tower, I knew interruptions were strictly forbidden, but emergencies can't wait! He sat in stunned silence to the news, while airborne pilots awaited his direction. As reality sunk in, an ever suspicious Tim said, "Who is this?" But when he heard his typically under control wife wail like a kid who just dropped her ice cream cone, he realized it was me and this was for real.

The technician called a high-risk specialist into the room to prep me on what to expect from this now complicated pregnancy. I'm no dummy. I knew what this meant, and after I rattled off all the expected challenges that lay ahead, the doctor, thinking he was complimenting me, said:

"Boy, you sure are no Pollyanna, are you?"

It's not that I didn't want the blessing I was given. It's just that it would take me years to realize that having unexpected triplets is a blessing.

My mom told my brother and me over the years that we had twins in the family, but who understands what that really means? The phenomenon that occurred while trying for our second baby (mind you, just trying to do something nice for my husband) was that two eggs dropped and one split. Our triplets are two identical boys and a girl. I became the mother of four: Matt, Kelly, Scott, and Derek. What's that saying? "Life is what happens to us while we are making other plans?"

The joke was on me.

Four kids, my husband's name starts with 'T', and he wears a uniform. That tea leaf reader turned out to be no quack.

"We Did It"

We survived. I'm happy to say I still have my 1991 Celica convertible sports car (150,000 miles and counting), in fact, we used the car to teach all the kids how to drive a stick shift. We skipped the minivan and comfortably transported the car seats, friends, luggage, and a never-ending amount of groceries in our Toyota Sequoia. I continued to run my business, which has supplied our family with much-needed income over the years, and my husband still happily serves his country, having been deployed to combat five times over the years. Being a military family meant not having the benefit of relatives living nearby while raising our children. The six of us took on the world together.

I quickly had to learn how to manage a family of six and become a Mom to four individual people. My ears literally rang for years from the buzz of controlled chaos. Turns out, I actually had a hidden talent for running an organized, respectful home with four children. I spent years denying my innate abilities to nurture well-adjusted, independent children only to find out that the "Powers That Be" knew me better than I knew myself.

This uncommon journey I've had the privilege of being on has taught me that for generations, we've been parenting using flawed, outdated methods. It's been humbling having mentored so many other parents with the counterintuitive methods that worked for us, and then watching as those other parents experienced the same magical relief from conflict, stress, and turmoil.

The strategies I've developed and taught for over fifteen years will give you the same lasting results.

I write this book with the gift of time and perspective. If I could package the wisdom I've gained into a tiny box to give to you, this book would be that box.

Quick Words About Chapter Order, Gender Use, and Personal Examples

The chapters build upon each other. For that reason, I encourage you to read every chapter. However, you certainly can skip around to find a specific topic that might need your immediate attention.

From my experience with other parents, I have found that even if you feel you have a particular concept or personality trait fully understood or embodied, it's typically the areas we dismiss that end up being the one we need the most help with. I propose keeping an open mind and being willing to do honest work on self-awareness to yield your best results.

A word about gender usage. Since I have three boys and one girl, I wrote examples vacillating between he/she her/him, with some added thems in there for good measure. I hope it doesn't drive you crazy. It's what felt most comfortable for me while writing.

Lastly, I use my clients and my own kids as examples. All client names have been changed and you'll notice two of my four kids are mentioned by name more often. That is simply due to their particular personalities. Our oldest takes the most hits. Poor guy has so many examples that apply to him, but we all cut our parenting teeth on our first born. Don't worry, he gladly approved!

Introduction

Your Child is the Result of How You Parent

"The trick is to care about everyone while not caring what they think."
~ Laughing Buddha Cafe

The material shared in this book originated from the trenches. I'm a real Mom, living real life, navigating real parenting challenges, just like you. I'm somewhat of an unconventional thinker when it comes to parenting. I'm sure my nonconformity is a result of having an enthusiastic interest in sophomoric comedy, swearing like a sailor, unapologetically speaking my mind, and tuning into the big picture when the daily grind bears down on me. These attributes have saved me from having a nervous breakdown on numerous occasions. Don't worry, though. Even if you don't have those traits, you can still stop the overwhelm and learn how to save yourself from parenting stress.

With a gaggle of kids in tow, I was now the Mom whose kids some teenager might want to trip in a restaurant. In fact, many times when we walked into a restaurant with all six of us, other diners groaned loudly as they saw four little kids about to be seated near them. How satisfying it felt when those same groaners came to our table after dinner and accused us of drugging our kids because they were so well behaved.

Over the past two decades, there were potential catastrophes in every event with four kids so close in age. I did get my ass kicked on occasion, but gradually I became more in touch with the natural parenting instincts I had no idea I possessed.

As those instincts became further refined, eventually friends began asking me for advice. I found myself in the unlikely position of being the go-to person to share tips, techniques, and parenting solutions. And I loved it. I happily and willingly dropped everything and carved out time to help guide a fellow parent through the challenges of raising kids. Through my natural evolution of helping friends, and friends of friends, and even strangers in supermarkets, I found my calling. Me, the one who never wanted kids, had become a parenting mentor!

As my clientele grew, what was a side-hustle became a full-time mentoring venture. I've worked with many parents whose stories will be throughout this book (names changed) and now I have the pleasure of mentoring parents every day through my Ask Mom platform.

The tactics I developed in the trenches are time tested. These are common sense practices, yet new revelations to the parents I work with. Every time a parent comes to me with their current huge problem, or a seemingly insurmountable chasm between them and their child, we go over a few questions then develop simple steps to solve their situation. They usually walk away from me a little skeptical that my often contradictory suggestion is going to work. Then, soon enough, those same people come back with their exciting story about how quickly and easily their situation has changed. One of my favorite pieces of parent feedback is – "I took a risk in going against what I thought I was supposed to do, and that's when the magic happened."

At some point we've all said, "No one ever hands us a book on how to raise kids." And yet, bookstore shelves are lined with stacks of them, each with its own set of do's and don'ts. *Secrets to Parenting Without Giving a F^ck* promises to impart reliable secrets, examples, and practical strategies so you can stop feeling parental overwhelm and develop happy humans.

My intention is to help you create your own style of parenting based on the tenets taught in this book. You will be able to raise your child successfully from ages 2-20, or any place in between. This material transcends the generational issues of the moment: gaming, the tech explosion, social media, and any future unknown trend kids will latch onto. The underlying approach is relatively the same for all situations; it's the primer from which all your parental responses and decisions will originate.

Secrets to Parenting Without Giving a F^ck takes practice. It takes a conscious willingness to ignore the noise and listen to your instincts.

Believe it or not, getting your mind to a state of give-less-of-a-f^ckness is where you strike that balance of being willing to learn while also staying committed to what you believe in. It takes grit, but you'll experience a rhythm once you get there and your kids will be on their way to becoming well-adjusted, independent thinkers.

Your first step toward parenting without giving a f^ck is being willing to change yourself. That may seem illogical: if you are not supposed to give a f^ck, why should you be the one changing? But know this: **Change Yourself and Your Child Changes.** When you change, kids respond.

Your child is the result of how you parent! There's always been one revelation about rebellious kids that has stood out like a blinking beacon: **Parenting is not about your child; parenting is about you**.

I'm teaching parents how to change *their* behavior; not *fix* their child's. Read that sentence again. The relationship you have with your child is up to you. As parents tweak their actions, their child's actions are affected. It takes some time to realize: *You are not reacting to your child, your child is reacting to you!*

You set the tone, you determine how your home is run, you decide how you react to your child's behavior, and you craft what kind of role model your child emulates every day. This is the mindset for parenting. You are in the parental driver's seat. You are the family CEO! With that VIP title comes the bonus that you are the leader and you own the culture of your home. Whichever way you veer, your family will follow. Flipping the switch to adopt this way of thinking requires that you buy-in to the basic philosophy that you want to raise a mentally resilient, self-sustaining child: a child who will thrive enthusiastically on his own, a child who will work through disappointment, fear, and mistakes without your constant intervention.

Making even the most miniscule adjustment to what you are doing now will result in fundamental and far-reaching improvements to your child's behavior. All it takes is being willing to learn this new approach and shake up your routine a bit.

Your perspective and attitude are something you have control over. Everyone can do this. Whoever you are, whoever your kids are, you can do this. This information is applicable no matter your child's skills, gifts, or needs. What you will learn in this book is suitable to all kids and to all people who care for children, not just parents—foster parents, teachers, guardians, and grandparents.

One of the most significant thought shifts you will experience from this book is: Kids are **"adults in training."** This parenting philosophy is woven into the fabric of every strategy, concept, or approach I teach. Recognizing your child as an adult in training provides a safety net from afar but does not solve your child's problems or punish your child for mistakes. As a parent, you want to create a simulated real-life environment in your home. This means telling your child phrases like: "Life isn't fair," "I'm sorry that happened to you," "How do you think you will handle that?" or, "Wake up earlier if you wanted that last Pop Tart." Parents should provide guidance, emotional support, and leadership when it's really needed, but we don't exist to swoop in to soothe our child's every discomfort. Kids are in training to become self-sustaining adults.

Introspection Prior to Changing Ourselves

Before I knew anything about being a parent, I had the instinct to consider my past and give thought to the kind of person I have been, and want to become, as a parent. I realized I would have some kind of influence on my child and so I put thought into the person my child would get to know as his mother. It was obvious that person might want to spruce herself up a bit.

When I became pregnant, my friends were scared for my unborn child. "Sue, you better clean up your act. You can't swear so much and have your infantile sense of humor with a kid around!"

Leaving the hospital with our first baby, it struck me that I held this little bundle of a blank slate who depended on me to guide, love, discipline, and advise him. It felt frightening and like tremendous pressure.

Of course I wanted to be a good parent and role model, but how much would I need to change myself to achieve parenting goddessness? Did I want to spend my life being a phony vanilla version of myself just because I now have a child? If I have to become bland and uptight to be considered a good parent, then where will it end? Should I also not participate in the magic of Santa, the Easter Bunny, or the Tooth Fairy because we can't live a little white lie?

I proudly decided I'd approach this new frontier as my bold, trash talking, crazy self. This child will know me for me and all my mistakes, past experiences, and embarrassing blemishes. No hiding, faking, or pretending. I will be my authentic self. That was the beginning of my unwitting venture into mindful parenting.

You get to attentively, consciously determine the kind of parent you want to be, and then become and be that parent daily. You will find a way to strike that balance between being truly you and being open to change where needed. Your influence is everything to your child and your changes directly result in your child's changes. You write the playbook and they adapt it.

So when the time came for my kids to question me about my stress-relieving foul mouth, I said, "Those are adult words. You may use them when you are an adult." That actually worked! At least until they were thirteen, and by then I had so many other landmines to avoid I didn't care if an occasional swear word slipped out.

In fact, allowing a tactical swear word was a parenting technique I used as incentive during extenuating circumstances. Specifically, I remember the time we all had our bellies full from a huge pancake breakfast and decided to go hiking directly after eating. Tim suggested beginning our climb up the steepest part of the hill (typical military guy,) and, predictably, a quarter of the way up the kids were doubled over with cramps. With four little ones complaining and crying, I redirected by allowing each one a swear word of their choice to repeat until we got to the top of the hill. You can't believe how useful that idea proved! Not to mention inappropriately funny.

Even though I decided to keep some of my more controversial personality traits, I also realized a few things about me needed to change. Being a mindful parent forces you to ask yourself the hard questions: "Why did I do that or say that? What previously held beliefs caused me to react that way? Am I happy with the result? If not, I have the power to choose different reactions with better results." I've learned that when I changed myself for the better, my kids changed for the better. Allowing for introspection, you will have the ways and means of having beautifully functioning relationships with your kids.

Having a great childhood myself likely helped prepare me for being a parent, but I still needed to do it all my own way, a bit differently than my parents. I had to create the mindset I needed to make life run the way I wanted it to.

I came into this parenting gig with some baggage of my own. For example, I lied all the time to my Mom, about everything. I thought deeply about why I lied so much. I recalled being punished quite a bit and forced to write, "I will not lie" 250 times while being grounded in my room for several days (it was the 70s.)

With the benefit of years behind me, I realized lying was about control. I didn't want to be told what to do. The only control I had as a child was to create my own environment by lying. The stricter my Mom acted, the more I lied. The more she punished me with grounding or snooped through my stuff, the more I became resolved in manipulating our interactions. Being punished reinforced my will and ability to lie even better to where I eventually put this skill to good use by having a marvelously successful career in sales!

It took a willingness for me to look inside, to be honest with myself, and not repeat the methods I knew wouldn't work. I had to change. I couldn't rely on the knee-jerk reactions of my upbringing.

In Part One, you will develop traits of your own to be a great parent without giving too many f^cks. You'll reconnect with your own self-worth, outside being a parent, and redefine your happiness through your own eyes. You'll learn how to parent with consistency, how to utilize personal discipline, and how to hone your ability to anticipate behaviors from your kids. Refreshing your relationship with yourself first allows you to become the parent your child needs you to be. Part One shows you how to leave behind old patterns and habits that aren't serving you as a parent.

Being agreeable to edifying yourself enables you to show up better for your kids. Doing self-work to have less ego, control, guilt, and shame will not only fortify you, but it will benefit you by leading you out of frustration and into fulfillment. When the adult is happy, the kid is happy. And the adult will be happy because the adult will be learning how to quickly, easily invite better behavior from their child in Part Two. You will be given the actual tools to raise well-adjusted, independent kids who love spending time with you and who add value to your life and to society.

If you can feel the possibility of your mind opening, then the first tenet of this parenting mindset is already working its magic. The days of public meltdowns, whining, not listening, lying, etc., will be in the past.

CASE STUDY – Your Child is the Result of How You Parent

Mom: Kate. 4 Sons: 10, 10, 6, 4

Kate was one of my earliest clients. She came to me for help over 10 years ago when she was at her wits end. She and her husband Jared had 4 active sons; twins Michael and Matthew who were 10, 6-year old Jacob, and Adam who was about to turn 4. Kate felt like overall she was doing pretty well as the mother of super active twin boys, and she even felt like she handled things well when Jacob got added to the mix. Once Adam came along, she felt like she lost control. Kate, like many parents, relied on using time-outs to calm the boys when they became too rambunctious. Her standard parenting M.O. when the boys got a little too crazy, or started fighting with each other, was to call a time-out. This method worked well initially. Her home went from chaos to quiet instantly for a few moments of peace and quiet. Kate became pretty comfortable with this pattern of escalation -- time out -- peace and quiet -- reboot -- rinse, repeat.

Then along came Adam. He took rowdy behavior to a whole new level. He began throwing tantrums and throwing food. Suddenly, Kate became faced with the reality of a child in full blown meltdown mode. A time-out would not be nearly enough to help bring peace when her child is throwing his dinner at the wall. A time out doesn't clean a wall dripping with food. She hated herself for thinking Adam might just be a "bad kid."

The very first insight I helped Kate understand is, it's *her* behavior, not Adam's, that allowed the problem to persist. Her ten-year practice of relying on time-outs only bought her a few moments of no yelling and running around, it didn't result in *teaching* the boys not to return to the behavior. Kate needed to recognize the control she thought she had before Adam was just an illusion. It's not that her method didn't work with Adam, the reality was it had never really worked at all! Because no bad behavior truly changed, it just briefly paused.

The way around this was for us to address the authority Kate forgot she had. After giving Kate clear steps to address how *she* responded to the rambunctious chaos, she learned to embrace that the power was within her, and her new responses, changed her child's actions. In addition to getting new creative alternatives to use as responses when her boys' energetic behavior ramped up, she also began feeling more under control knowing her kids responded to her reactions. Kate quickly began getting results that became permanent changes to how the boys behaved in the house. Within three days of our first session, Adam's food throwing habit stopped, and within two weeks his tantrums all but disappeared. Parent-directed time-outs were never needed again. Kate became empowered in her approach and quickly found her life much less chaotic. Kate changed herself first and watched in awe as her kids changed.

PART ONE

YOUR RELATIONSHIP WITH YOURSELF

Chapter 1

Ego; Checked.

"I have my faults. But being wrong isn't one of them." ~ Jimmy Hoffa

Having been a woman addicted to control most of her life, I naturally expected my kids to fall in line by just telling them once what I wanted them to do. Our firstborn, Matt, could sniff weakness from a mile away. One false move or hesitation to correct his behavior and he exploited me. I yelled so much from frustration that my throat became sore and raspy. Yelling was all I knew how to do. Matt heard daily, "Do it because I said. Do it now and like it!" I thought it would be that easy. Yet no behavior ever changed as I yelled louder and more often. Matt's eyes glazed over as he tuned me right out.

Matt's personality characteristics would make him successful one day, but those same characteristics also made him difficult to parent. These characteristics included always wanting to be in control (props to Mom,) always needing explanations because there needs to be a reason, being ultra-confident for his age, and never meeting a rule he didn't want to break (head nod to Mom again.)

Combine a super-assertive firstborn with the addition of triplets, I soon grew sick and tired of shouting with no one listening. It reached a boiling point when my husband left for combat while I had four kids under age four. I was so exhausted I took cat naps at red lights. Desperate and at my wits end, I decided to attend a parenting class at the Montessori school where Matt attended kindergarten.

I sat in my first class with my ego fully locked and loaded, eyes readied for an abundance of rolling. *What was I even doing here? I didn't really need this, right?* Sure, I was yelling a lot, but I have most things under control. While discussing the first chapter of our book, the instructor asked me for an example of what I'd like to learn from this class. I answered, with a whiff of smugness, "Overall, I'm doing fine. If I had to pick something, I'd say my throat is sore from yelling too much, but I'm 100% justified. I have one and half-year-old triplets, a four-year-old wise guy, a husband deployed, a full-time business, and no friends or family in Boise as we just moved here."

I was certain she'd feel sorry for me, tell me to buy some cough drops, and realize I'm already doing an amazing job with all I have on my plate. Instead, after my laundry list of reasons validating why yelling is a justified parenting technique, the teacher asked a brilliant three-word question that sliced right through my ignorance and ego: **"Is it working?"**

Boom.

Shut down like a box of Twinkies at a Keto party. Screaming wasn't working. My list of justifications weren't valid reasons to scream at my kids. The teacher now had my undivided attention. Once I accepted my ego was in my way, preventing me from being open to new ideas, I dropped the walls and became more available in the class.

Learning happened quickly after that. Yelling stopped soon thereafter. I had more of a handle on daily life and I started listening to my kids more. And guess what? My kids followed suit.

Are your current techniques working for you?

Ego is Personal

Our ego is a mash-up of what we've been told about ourselves from others and our own perceptions of ourselves as they relate to the world around us. Those perceptions were developed as a defense mechanism from other people's opinions and observations. Our ego is a barrier our subconscious created to shield us from difficult truths and provide a justification for our negative behaviors.

In the name of protection, our ego creates a wall between us and our ability to listen and learn freely without reservation. Our ego makes us stubborn for no reason, closed to others' feelings and opinions, and it can make us feel insecure when there is no cause for it.

Negative emotions tied to ego are shame, blame, pride, and embarrassment. The ego is a complex, interlaced entity. Someone says something hurtful: we believe it, we build a wall, and those hurtful opinions become internalized as part of our psyche/ego. Who decides if we feel shame, blame, pride, or embarrassment? We do. We decide whether we let other people's opinions define us. When our ego makes the decisions, it skews our reality to however we want to view ourselves and however we want to make ourselves feel.

Like it's been said, there are three sides to every story—yours, mine, and the truth. In every exchange with another person, whether it's an adult or a child, our ego filters how we hear the other person's words. Our mind will let us think whatever feels good for us to believe. Our ego is really of *our own* creation. An identity we crafted for ourselves, our own personal myth.

Nothing exposes our ego like becoming a parent. For instance: I was rocking my 1980's bright argyle Benetton sweater one cold day. My daughter, about ten at the time, innocently asked if she could borrow my sweater the next day. "Of course." I could not have been more proud that my good taste had transcended decades and generations. She immediately followed with, "It's ugly sweater day!" I practically peed my pants laughing. To this day we have a hearty laugh over that moment. Just remember, if you can laugh when your child innocently cuts you to the core, you'll turn a potentially tough moment into a great memory.

Kids will find and capitalize on our every perceived flaw. I think most of us will admit that being parents has made us better people. We are more patient, more compassionate, and we are forced into becoming more flexible, whether we like it or not. Kids are our best and most influential teachers, *when we are willing to listen.* Humbling ourselves is appealing at any age.

During that first parenting class, I began my transition into becoming less ego-centric and more open to learning new approaches to parenting. When I felt justified in yelling at my kids and confused as to why I wasn't getting results, embarrassment, shame, pride, and blame were all served up on a silver platter. Husband gone to combat (blame,) screaming at my kids (shame, embarrassment,) just moved to Boise, have no friends (pride.) I needed to refresh my perspective. Understanding our ego from the context that it's a self-created façade gives us the power to know we can simply just decide to tune out the noise and choose not to internalize it.

Your Child's Ego Wall

If you are using any shame, blame, or embarrassment phrases as a parent, you contribute to the ego wall your child is building. He absorbs what you project and he is already constructing those walls to shield himself from the emotions those phrases evoke. You have the chance to break that cycle with responses that build him up. Give him choices without any hidden ego-agenda. Tailor your choices for his benefit, not to protect yourself. To help your child grow up without an unhealthy ego, start by raising him without yours in the way.

EXAMPLE - Parenting with shame, blame, and embarrassment

Think for a minute about how your ego drives your parenting.

Do you shame to get results?

"You're a naughty girl. I told you to pick up your toys."
"Don't be so selfish. Share with your brother."

Do you blame to get results?

"If you hadn't slept so late, we'd be on time."

Do you embarrass to get results?

"Yikes, you're wearing stripes and plaid. That doesn't match."

Unrealized Dreams and Ego

Do you attempt to live out your own unfulfilled, unaccomplished life goals through your child? "Get straight A's, play football, become a lawyer." Even though you didn't get straight A's, play ball, or become a lawyer. If you're doing this, it's all ego talking.

The Things We Say Matter

It's crushing when I overhear a parent call their child names or attach a condescending label to them whether it be at a store or at a friend's house. For example, when a child does something silly or makes a mistake and a parent says, "What are you, stupid?" or, "That was dumb; why do you say dumb things?" Under the guise of being funny, mean words are spoken and they accrue to become part of the child's narrative. It's never funny to call someone names or say, "Shut up." With my own kids, I'll allow "shit" all day, but "shut up" or "stupid?" Now I'm involved.

Ways to Reinforce a Healthy Ego in Your Child

All this talk about ego-checking might appear as if I think egos are a bad thing. Quite the contrary. We all have one. My point with this chapter is to reiterate that, unless you've resolved your own ego's imbalances, it's not realistic to think you can help your child develop his in a healthy way. The extent to which you have your ego's edges softened is in direct proportion to your ability to nurture your child's.

Kids imitate what their parents do. How you handle challenges, solve problems, and take accountability without blaming others will show your child how to act. Stepping up to take ownership is one of the most important things we can teach ourselves and our children. That kind of self-ownership helps maintain healthy egos for both yourself and your child.

A simple way to keep your child's ego balanced is to keep your own ego *about them* in balance. In other words, let them develop as an original, unique person in your eyes, not an extension of you or a reflection of you. It's important to remind yourself not to compare your child to other siblings, friends, yourself, or anyone. It's not about who they are similar to or different from: it's about who they are.

So many times I found myself mentally comparing whichever child I was engaged with to either myself or to my brother or my husband's family. While kids may like knowing they share similarities to family members, to help keep the child's individual ego intact, we need to see the present person before us and not draw similarities and conclusions that prevent them from being their original selves.

If we take the time to support their ideas, thoughts, and concerns with no judgment, our kids experience themselves as contributors to the family. That feeling translates to building their self-confidence outside the family because they feel they add value. With our own adult ego in balance, we better guide our child to keeping his in balance.

It's Nobody Else's Business

If you wonder what others will think of you if your child talks or acts a certain way, then here is a way to put an end to worrying about what others think. **Stick with the facts, not others' opinions.**

My favorite way to look at this is through the Four F's; if someone isn't Feeding you, Funding you, Fixing things for you, or Fucking you, then you shouldn't give a damn what they think.

Any need for your self-preservation will get in the way of boosting your child's self-esteem. If you're busy saving face, you won't be focused on how you can truly support your child in the situation. Your ego creates a barrier toward having a deeper relationship with your child. Opportunities are lost and beautiful memories are never made, all due to a bruised adult ego.

CASE STUDY – Ego
Mom: Bella. 2 Daughters: 6, 8

Bella is a single mom, working long hours, raising two daughters. When we met, the first thing she said to me through her tears was "I'm yelling so loud at my girls that my neighbor says she can hear me!" Bella is a sweet person, and a really devoted Mom, but she is also exhausted much of the time, and gets easily exasperated when her girls leave a mess every day and fight with each other. When her neighbor told her that she could hear her yelling, Bella was mortified, but it also became clear to me she felt the yelling might be justified. "They don't listen and I have no choice but to yell at them even though nothing ever changes." I saw immediately Bella's ego was doing the talking…or, in this case, the yelling.

After asking Bella some questions designed to help her step back and notice what's really happening, she quickly realized how *her yelling contributed* to her daughters' ongoing behavior. She opened up to the possibility that maybe it wasn't her daughters' fault after all, maybe with a different ego-less approach she could get different results. Once Bella recognized her repeated actions spurred her daughters' repeated actions, she concluded that trying a new and unexpected idea might get better results. We agreed on strategies for her to apply with the girls, to interrupt the behavior cycle. We also agreed on methods to raise her awareness and her ability to recognize where her ego was "doing the talking" and to recognize her triggers so she could minimize over-reactions. Further, we established techniques for self-care to help her develop a more balanced way of looking at her role as a Mom. I'm happy to say that Bella has not cried since our first meeting, and, by all reports, she hasn't yelled either!

Ego Self-Reflections

Ask yourself, as if in front of a mirror and with no fear, to face the truth of what you bring to the relationship:

1. Have you ever used shame or blame language to motivate your child?
2. Are you willing to learn new things from your child?
    a. If not, why not?
    b. If so, what has your child taught you?
3. Do you have a tendency to take situations with your child personally?
4. When you act, is it about your child or about making yourself feel better?
5. How much time do you spend considering what other people think about you or your child?

Ego Gamechangers

1. List three to five things you currently do that you want to change in the way you interact with your children.
2. Identify any ego challenges in your relationship with your kids.
3. Identify where other people's opinions of your children concern you. What makes their opinion important?

Takeaway Tool:

Is what you're doing working?

Chapter 2

How to Let Go of Control & Trust Your Gut

"Parenting was so much easier when I raised my non-existent children hypothetically."
~ Anonymous

I experienced many epiphanies on my parenting journey, and learning to let go of control was among the first and most impactful. With 100% certainty, I can tell you that life on the other side of being controlling is like the difference between a black and white photo and an illuming image on the cover of *National Geographic*. It's vibrant and freeing and it made me unexpectedly happy.

Here is the epiphany: lose control to gain control.

Letting go of the need to control my kids took awareness, and the willingness to work at it, but to my shock, it led to rapidly improved behavior from my children. Not to mention, once I started to get the hang of it, it spread into other relationships. My hubby and even my work colleagues were all loving the new, non-controlling me.

Letting go of control doesn't come easy. It's a process.

First, I needed to admit my controlling ways to myself and recognize that no one in my sphere, including my kids, wanted to be bossed.

Second, I had to redefine the actual "need" factor as it applied to my involvement in any situation.

Third, I honed and connected with my intuition and instincts to trust myself and the journey we are all independently living.

Admit It. Here's How We Justify Being Controlling

In my black and white picture life, I had myself convinced I needed to manage and control every situation and, by extension, the people involved, for events to work out as I thought they should. I needed my kids to do what I said, do it right, and be happy I asked! When they didn't do it "right" I fell into the old adage, "If you want it done right, do it yourself." Sound familiar?

Gradually, I figured out there are many ways to get any job done. Of course, teaching kids to be independent at a young age takes patience and acceptance of sub-par results, but that's the price we pay for instilling independence into our children. If we have the need to control our kids, their actions, and the outcomes, it will backfire eventually, I guarantee it. Just ask the kid who is lying to his parents or the kid who would rather be at his friend's house than at his own home. Just for the record, if you don't outgrow this, you'll still be trying to control your kids when they are fully grown adults, and that *never* goes over well.

Here's a counter-intuitive and powerful fact: controlling actions from parents are the anti-good behavior tool. We start out with the best intentions, thinking we are doing the right thing, being involved and a good parent. But, sure as shit, we will be in fisticuffs with our kids daily if we control them with "empty the trash now; rinse your dishes this minute." Every time we utter a controlling sentence we encourage a power struggle.

We create a difficult situation for ourselves when we force or demand our child do something. The balance of power inevitably ends up in our child's hands. We want to avoid backing our child into a corner to where he can just say, "No, I'm not doing it." Typically, it starts with our controlling demand, which leads to our child deciding to show us he has the power to say no. We respond with some form of punishment (more control on top of control) and it all ends in a power struggle that can easily be avoided by rephrasing our requests.

We find ourselves controlling situations that won't even matter a month or two after the event. If we step back, the situation will usually resolve itself on its own, without any input from us. If we constantly get involved, it makes our child feel resentful and trapped. He doesn't want to be dependent on us. He wants to be independent and we want him to be independent, but we are in the way.

Being controlling is a completely unnecessary burden we put on ourselves. If we have too big of a stake in the outcome of any event, or we are unwilling to compromise because we always know what's best, then we are being needlessly controlling. If we are the parent who is involved in every transaction between our child and his teacher or we are convinced he needs our help to get better grades or to have the best looking school project, then we are being needlessly controlling. If we find ourselves emailing his coach because he isn't getting enough playtime on the field, then we are being needlessly controlling. Let go of it. All of it. Kids figure life out and become self-confident in the process.

Checklist to Identify Controlling Behavior:

- ❑ Do I need to be right or be the hero or rescuer?
- ❑ Do I want to say, "I told you so?"
- ❑ Do I mask using control by hiding behind safety? "You can't go; it's not safe."
- ❑ Do I have a need to be needed?
- ❑ Am I helping or controlling by doing it for them?
- ❑ Who is benefiting from my involvement, me or my child?

Checklist to Identify Non-Controlling Behavior

- ❑ I am acting as facilitator.
- ❑ I do not have an agenda other than my child's best interest.
- ❑ I am providing resources and support.
- ❑ I am providing a safe environment for them to make choices.
- ❑ I provide structure and consistency.
- ❑ My child has clear boundaries and limits and can trust that they have freedom within those stated limits.

Give Them Choices

One quick strategy for starting to give them control is to structure your phrases so your child gets to make as many decisions as she can. "What book do you want to read tonight?" "What outfit do you want to wear today?" "What after school activity do you want to do?" That's how she learns to advocate for herself. Every decision she makes leads to a new experience and new experiences are the foundation to her growth and development.

Redefining the "Need" Factor

During my controlling black and white photo days, I felt truly burdened by the sheer amount of needs placed on me by having a family. Among the many daily chores were: washing and sorting laundry for four kids; planning, shopping and preparing breakfasts, lunches and dinners; cleaning the house; etc. Day, after day, after day, after day.

Guess what? The reality is, we are actually needed a tiny fraction of the times we think we are. I was matter-of-factly informed of that at a Montessori parent/teacher conference when the triplets were four years old. As I ran late for my timeslot, I wiped imaginary sweat from my brow, exasperated from being so damn needed. "Sorry I'm late, as you can imagine, making four breakfasts, packing four lunches, and cleaning up after them—it's just overwhelming every morning." I admitted getting pissed off when it took even longer (every second counts during the A.M. routine) because the kids didn't answer me on what flavor juice they wanted. "Kelly, grape or fruit punch? Kelly! Scott, grape or fruit? UGH, I'll just pick for you, but you better not complain."

The teacher, with complete disinterest in my sweaty brow theatrics, schooled me as to all the things my kids can and do accomplish in their classrooms. She started with, "Why are you still making their lunches?" At first, I thought this Grandma-aged teacher must have forgotten the daily grind! Why *wouldn't* I be making their lunches? They're four! Then she continued, "They self-initiate and manage all friend disagreements on a 'peace rug,' they grind coffee and make art out of it, they put snack menus together and then serve their class, they put all items back where they got them and they serve as role models and leaders to the two and three year old's." Wow! My kids were doing all of that and much more every day at school. Why convince myself I had to do so much for them at home?

That teacher first opened my eyes to the fact I undermined them by doing everything for them. The kids became as frustrated by my annoying juice flavor questions as I was by their lack of snap-to-it appreciation for all I kept doing for them. Well, you don't have to tell me twice!

From that day forward, they made their own lunches. I cut the fruit and put snacks, meat, bread at their eye level. I made sure Ziploc bags and lunch boxes were available and clean. They picked their own flavor juice, made their sandwiches or packed dinner leftovers, selected their fruit and were in charge of creating the shopping list when something ran out. Best of all they *loved* doing it.

I got so energized by this new realization of their capabilities, we bought them their own pop up hampers and all four kids began doing their own laundry. Gone were the days of holding up boys' shirts and asking wearily, "Whose is this one?"

We trained and supervised them in each new task, but once they learned it, I let go of thinking they needed me for that task. This led to the kids doing even more around the house (they took out garbage, washed and changed sheets, and kept rooms clean) as I let go of the reins. Life became less overwhelming. I no longer felt like everything depended so much on me. My black and white photo started to fill in with some color again. Bonus: as I felt less burdened, my kids felt trusted and independent. Even through high school, they celebrated packing their own lunches and doing their own laundry. Throughout their school years, they'd come home and say, "Mom, I can't believe so-and-so still has his Mom pack his lunch. He throws away half of it!"

PS: *Yes, it's true. Kids throw away or give away your lovingly packed lunches because they didn't choose it; you did.*

How Connecting to Your Intuition Helps You Let Go of Control

I am a huge believer in intuition, in trusting your gut. Being raised in a half Italian family, intuition served as a highly prized and openly acknowledged skill that we all had. Of course, you don't need to be Italian to rely on your intuition, your inner knowing, or your gut instinct. We all have intuition, we just don't all listen to it to the same degree. Your willingness to let go of control is what allows your inner voice to talk to you and allows you to listen unencumbered. We tend to distrust our intuitive messages, dismiss our inner knowing, or shove our gut feelings aside because we don't have facts to back them up. But as we let go of control our inner voice will get louder. And if we listen, we can develop a vital trust in our instincts and trust in ourselves. Once we relax control and start trusting ourselves, our parenting becomes much more purposeful.

Not only did my intuitive instincts sharpen as I let go of control, but I recognized each of my children for the individual they are. Each of them had their own intuitive instincts they would need to rely on someday. But they couldn't develop those instincts if I didn't allow them to. Having controlling parents shut down their natural journey of liberation and self-determination.

Each of our children is their own unique soul, infused with their own innate gifts and passions that will allow them to make their own distinct impact in the world. It's tempting to consider our children to be "ours," but we don't have ownership over anyone. We are all on our own personal journey, us and our children. No one should have control over anyone else's journey. Just because we are the parent, it doesn't give us the right to control our child. Our children are already complete humans. Our role is to foster the enriching environment that paves their way.

Many times it was challenging trusting that a situation would resolve itself without my commanding it to be resolved. Those are the times when it's critical that you not only learn to trust your gut, but also allow your child to trust theirs. If you really want your bestie's kid to be best friends with yours, but your child resists, there isn't anything you can do. Honor their instincts.

Letting Them Pick Their Friends

A particular friend of our son checked every box of what you don't want your child exposed to (sneaking out, wanting to act like an adult way before it's time, sex way too young, playing with a parent's hidden gun.) Yet, we knew that if we forbade the friendship, it would make that friend all the more alluring.

We trusted our instincts, and our son's, that he would find his way, and he did. Don't get me wrong, we watched like a hawk, more than our son knew, but didn't exert control or impose uncharacteristic restrictions. These two grew up together from five years old: there was history there. As his friend veered in a different direction, we still felt full confidence in our son's ability to make sensible decisions for himself. We based this confidence on our son's actions. He kept us informed with detailed honesty, which we rewarded via continued trust. His open communication gave us the chance to teach, share ideas, and keep tabs on how bad things were getting with his friend. As long as communication stayed open, curfew stayed on time, and no other odd behavior crept in, we were good. If we saw our son becoming secretive, not sharing openly with us, or curfew became an issue, we would have gotten involved. By resisting that urge initially, trusting our child and watching how he handles situations, he typically made good choices. In the back of our minds though, we kept in mind that he was an adult in training and were ready to step in if actions changed. Specific details about how we would have stepped in are all throughout Part Two.

Eventually, I became grateful for that friend. He gave us a chance to discuss the important topics of gun safety, curfew, and sex with each of our kids as a family at dinner. Most challenges offer golden opportunities for teachable moments. Unless, of course, you are busy living in fear and controlling those moments. Then you miss the chance to turn them into life lessons for your kids.

Letting Them Find Their Own Purpose and Passions

You may have a child who has the voice of an angel and could be singing professionally. Singing makes her happy. She sings whenever she's upset to cheer herself up. She even sings conversations. You deeply believe it could be her life's purpose. Yet she may not even be close to recognizing that gift in herself. You can't make that realization occur any faster. She has to live life's experiences for herself and grow confident in her own abilities. No amount of control will change that, or make any child find their personal purpose any faster. Trust your instinct and trust life's process as a parent without controlling it.

We don't have the right to assume, choose, or control our child's life purpose. Just like you wouldn't want anyone having control over your life's purpose. Children face their own personal growth in their own way, in their own time. As a parent, we serve as guides to help facilitate life lessons by providing resources and opportunities for choices. Our job is to provide safety and security. We need to release our personal attachment whenever possible.

Letting Your Child Find Their Own Heroes

Kids reach a point where they need to start having experiences with outside sources to reinforce the lessons you teach at home. They need to come into contact with coaches, teachers, friends, parents of friends, and bosses. When the time is right, say to your child, "You are on your own journey. You will meet the people you need to meet who will further you on your personal path, those who will help you figure out your purpose for being on this earth." I told our kids that phrase many times once I felt my messages had already gotten through or were being tuned out. Typically, my gut feelings are what told me when it was time for our kids to start hearing different perspectives from other people. The age when this happens is different for every child. The right time to peel yourself away will likely be instinctual, if you've been working on listening to your gut.

Most people have had that one teacher or coach or boss who took a special interest in them and who exposed them to a new unforeseen opportunity. Have trust in yourself as the parent to know you serve a vitally important role in your child's life. You are irreplaceable. Don't feel threatened by her having other key figures in her life. By allowing and encouraging those relationships, you actually become even more irreplaceable to her. There is no need to hover or limit those interactions. You will be the yardstick by which she compares all outside opinions. Let her be exposed to other people and opinions and you will be the one she discusses them with while she formulates her own ideas.

At every age, our parenting challenge is figuring out when to teach, when to step back, and when to intervene. By being engaged, connecting to your intuition, and letting go of the need to control, you will know when to teach and correct and when to let it pass. But you must listen. Progress in life is only possible because of challenges, and sometimes the best thing you can do for your child is let them experience the challenge without your intervention. When we let go of control while providing safety, consistency, support, and the resources they need, we allow our children to develop their ability to make choices, build their self-esteem, and their trust in their own intuition. The more you listen to your own intuition and the more you allow your child to exercise and develop their own intuition, the stronger individuals you both will become.

CASE STUDY – Control

Mom: Ashlyn. 1 Son: 11

Ashlyn is divorced and sharing custody of her 11-year old son, John, with her ex-husband. Ashlyn's best friend was a client of mine and suggested she talk with me about her concerns for John. Ashlyn became deeply concerned John wasn't making friends. "He's just not socializing. He's bored and lonely, and I'm really worried about him." She tried hard to encourage him to have friends over. She told me of one of John's friends from school she particularly liked, but John resisted having him over. John told Ashlyn he had a bad feeling about this kid but didn't really know why. The more Ashlyn pushed, the more frustrated they both got, and the more confused and depressed John seemed.

I could literally see the shock in Ashlyn's eyes when my first question was, "What makes you think he's lonely?" Her eyes got even bigger with my second question, "Have you considered honoring your son's instincts?" It never occurred to Ashlyn she might be making huge assumptions about her son's behavior, or her own. She assumed because he doesn't share her same interests in people or even her same opinion about specific people that he's not socializing. She assumed when he's alone with her, he's lonely and bored. She never considered trusting him and his instincts. He gave her very clear feedback he felt something off with this other kid, but she saw that as a sign something was wrong with John and pushed him to go against his instinct.

Once Ashlyn became aware of how limiting her control could be on John's developing instincts and decision-making abilities she began to let go and trust him. She stopped inserting her involvement in unnecessary situations and unexpected magic happened. As her son felt more freedom to make his own choices, they started to hang out and talk more. It was then that Ashlyn learned the real root of John's behavior. He admitted his mom's home was a source of comfort for him, and he preferred one-on-one time with his mom, to the distraction of friends. John and Ashlyn developed a much more open, close relationship than Ashlyn ever thought possible. Her control and assumptions could have prevented such a beautiful possibility.

Control Self-Reflections

1. Are you frustrated or exhausted by everything you think you have to do for your kids?
2. Are you comfortable being wrong or not knowing all the answers?
3. Do you like being the hero? What would happen if you didn't rescue your kids?
4. Do you ever say no because you're afraid your child won't make the right decision?
5. Do you ever get involved or help when it's truly not needed? Why?

Control Gamechangers

1. What things do you think you have to do for your child that contribute to you feeling overwhelmed? (i.e.: doing laundry, driving them around, helping them fulfill their commitments, etc.)
2. Keep track for one week of all the times you say "No." Keep a list of every time you hear yourself say it, big and small.
    a. Go over the list and note which times were out of convenience.
    b. Which were stated as a safety issue and note if it really was.
    c. Which were because you thought you had to be involved, but you really didn't?

d. Which were taking away their chance to make a choice?

e. Which were because you did not trust them?

Visualization

What version of hands below best represent how you parent when you feel scared, frustrated, or impatient?

Open = Permissive

Clenched = Controlling

Cupped = Open with Support

Takeaway Tool

Listen, guide, let them decide.

Chapter 3

Why Guilt Is a Wasted Emotion

"It's only a problem if it's a problem for you."
~ Anonymous

In the midst of daily parenting, we make thousands of decisions a day. Many of them are on the fly and involve subjects we have zero experience managing. Each day brings different challenges we've never faced before. There's no good reason to experience guilt under these circumstances; we all are doing the best we can while facing the onslaught of unfamiliarity.

Guilt can lead to making emotional decisions instead of practical ones. Guilt can hold us hostage to other's motivations. Guilt is a toxic cycle of decision, regret, and beating ourselves up (shame.) Personally, I like myself too much to hold myself to the immense pressure of always handling situations in the exact correct way. When I've done something regrettable, I just tell myself, "I'll do it better tomorrow." I let myself off the hook. Guilt is like having a third boob. It serves no other purpose than to make you feel weird and wrong.

Admittedly, I might be a little different than most people when it comes to guilt. I have made it my practice to consciously choose not to process feelings of guilt or let it seep into my life. I do this in two ways. One, I don't second-guess my decisions once I've made them. If careful consideration has gone into the decision, there's no need to doubt myself. If I make a mistake, I simply apologize or correct it. Two, I don't live a life of regret. If my intentions are pure and I have done my best, I choose not to let myself feel regret.

You might wonder, "How can I tell myself not to experience guilt?" The first step is to notice whether you naturally resort to feeling guilty when your child is upset. Do you automatically assume it's because of you or assume you can make it better by overcompensating in some other way? After recognizing that feeling, the second step is to form the habit of releasing it because you know it's unproductive to be angry with yourself over a situation you have the ability to change with an apology or with clarification.

Self-reflect on the times when you may already not be taking on guilt or where you easily put your foot down and translate those situations into being applicable to your kids. For example, maybe you excel at standing up for yourself and telling someone "no" when needed. Conversely, maybe your house isn't so clean one day. It's full of dog hair and toys everywhere when someone stops by unannounced. This makes you wracked with guilt over what this person must be thinking about you.

Figure out what's different between both scenarios for you, one where you put your foot down, easily saying no, and the other where you suffer in a guilt grip over being judged about a messy home. Then examine the circumstances in both cases to understand what scenarios tend to elicit guilty feelings in you and what scenarios you can easily release. This self-analysis will help you understand how you process guilty feelings. Then, apply that to your parenting.

When Matt was young, he built self-designed, intricate fighter jets made from Legos. He often handed them to me so I could get a closer look. In my clumsiness, I'd inevitably break a few pieces off. I'd feel badly because he'd worked hours creating them, but when I looked him in the eye and said, "Mommy's sorry buddy, I'm left-handed and clumsy." He'd always say, "It's Okay, Mommy." He never stopped being brave enough to let me hold his creations.

Not experiencing guilt is a great parenting strength. It prevents you from being a prisoner of emotional warfare, where some parents find themselves trapped. Not allowing feelings of guilt will keep your momentum going without getting stuck in a self-defeatist attitude. Raising kids offers unending chances to tweak, adapt, and succeed. To avoid feelings of guilt, you can create the mental habit that with every decision you make, take note of how you responded and how it turned out. If tears, confusion, and pushback result, you tweak and adapt to new ideas. If happiness, eager behavior, and cooperation result, you succeed and build on it. When you admit and apologize for a mistake and quickly put it behind you, you teach your kids to do the same when they make a mistake.

Allowing yourself to feel guilt changes nothing. Guilt is not action based. It's an emotion that manifests in drama, passive aggressive comments, and the silent treatment. All are unrewarding emotional states that don't solve problems and won't deepen your relationship bonds.

End Guilt in Three Steps:

1. Ask yourself, "Was it me?"
2. If yes, apologize or clarify.
3. Tell yourself, "I'll do it better tomorrow." Then release it.

P.S. *Here's a little tip. I have found that kids' memories of day-to-day interactions don't form into something long-lasting until they are about 9+ years old. This is unscientific, of course, but based on my real-life experience. That means that you don't need to continually criticize yourself about all the little things you say or do that you think your child is hanging onto. They don't even remember by bedtime. And by the time they become teenagers, it's Mom and Dad, who?! All the day-to-day pain and anguish you spend feeling guilty is time wasted.*

The Four Categories of Guilt

1. The guilt you put onto yourself.
2. The guilt you put onto others (your kids.)
3. The guilt you allow your kids to put onto you.
4. The guilt you allow society to put onto you.

The guilt you put onto yourself: This type of guilt makes you prone to second-guessing yourself. It puts you in a weakened state. Typically, parents susceptible to this type of guilt aren't taken seriously and their rules are broken easily. Say your son comes home past curfew and you overreact by calling him names like 'irresponsible' and 'thoughtless.' You reacted emotionally and now you feel so guilty about what you said, you apologize profusely but never end up addressing the fact that he came home late. Now he has you pegged for being easily guilted and knows it's easy to distract you to the point of overlooking your rules.

Instead, tell him you are sorry you overreacted calling him irresponsible and thoughtless, those were words you regret using. The issue is curfew and his lack of respect for your rules. Remove the guilt by acknowledging your part (overreacting) and then you can deal productively with the behavior of breaking curfew.

What if you are late picking up your daughter from school? You feel badly you left her waiting by herself, so you overcompensate by driving her to school the next day, when she usually walks, and you get her a fast food dinner because you feel so guilt-ridden. Talk about trying too hard! All your daughter needs to hear is, "I'm so sorry I was late. That must have been scary wondering where I was." That's it. She doesn't need you overreacting and trying too hard to fix your honest mistake. It diminishes your parental status. Parents are people who make mistakes. We are busy, we work, we run a household, we have other kids. Shit happens. Sorry. She still walks to school tomorrow and she eats what's for dinner. She was planning to do that all along until your self-loathing got in the way.

The guilt you put onto others (your kids): This type of guilt creates resentment. Say you play the kids against one another. "Your older sister gets her homework done on time. Why can't you be more like her?" Or say you guilt your child into a desired action because you don't know how else to get her to do what you're asking. If you use guilt to get a certain behavior from your child. Ask yourself, "At what cost?"

Guilting your child causes bitterness and weakens your authority. For example, it's a Saturday night and you have a bad feeling about a party your daughter wants to attend. You want her to stay home so you politely ask her not to go, but she storms off accusing you of never letting her do anything. A guilt-inducing response would be: "If you love me, you'll stay home tonight." That might work once, but the cost you pay for getting her to listen with a guilt trip makes her experience you as emotionally weak. You just taught her that if someone makes her feel badly, she has to give that person attention. That leaves damage to her self-confidence. You've exploited her love for you to get her to do something for you. Guilt-using parents are vulnerable parents.

The guilt you allow your kids to put onto you: This type of guilt makes you susceptible to manipulation. Don't think your kids haven't figured that out. An example of this is: Your son's friend has the latest Xbox and the newest iPhone. He throws it in your face. He feels embarrassed. "Why don't love me as much as Joe's parents love him?" My favorite mantra to this type of conversation was two words: "Tough tits." My kids would be rich if they had a dollar for every time they heard me tell them "tough tits" as a response to their sob story about what any other family was doing, spending, or saying. Sometimes I'd switch it up to "tough ta-tas" just to keep it fresh.

Another example is if we missed a sports game, we respectfully reminded them we had to work or had another commitment, and we'd catch the next one. No hard feelings. Truth be told, they don't want you at every game, anyway. Kids need to be reminded that you have a life and it's not your job to meet their every perceived need. Remember, saying no to your child is not the same as hurting their feelings.

The guilt you allow society to put onto you: This type of guilt gives you feelings of inadequacy. The life you've created for yourself is enough for you and it's enough for your child. There is no right or wrong way; there's just what's right for you. You don't need buy-in and validation from family or friends on your decisions. Conversely, you don't need to concern yourself with the decisions other people make for their families. What's right for you is right. What's right for them is right. Period. No explanation needed.

Don't open yourself up to comparisons from other parents or from your kids about what other parents are doing. When your child has leadership from you, he knows the actions of other parents are not even a blip on your radar. Within the security of your leadership, he grows confident in his choices and he won't be susceptible to guilt from society or peers.

A Note About Gifts and Guilt

While we're on the subject of guilt, I'd like to share my personal, albeit controversial, opinion on gifts. Don't get me one. And don't expect me to get you one. The operative word here is expect. This opens up the door for lots of guilt if my gift or my schedule of giving does not meet expectations. Spontaneous gifts are lovely, but expected ones based on a designated holiday can get out of hand quickly. In parenting, obligatory gifts can establish an unbalanced set of expectations. It's easy for family giving to get out of control and lead to ever increasing expectations on you. When giving a gift to either your child, friend, or spouse, ask yourself: what emotion is attached to this gift? Is it control, is it for reciprocity, is it to be liked, or is it simply for their well-being? My greatest gift to my husband (and kids, friends, family) is they don't have to give me a gift. The thought of my family spending time, money, and effort shopping for a gift for me because the calendar says so is too much of a mandate. If you happen to see something I'd like and want to share it with me, that's wonderful. I will do the same. The best gift you can ever give anyone is your time. It's free and guilt-free…if you aren't giving it out of guilt!

CASE STUDY – Guilt

Mom: Emily. 1 Daughter, 8; 1 Son, 5

I knew Emily even before she came to me for parent mentoring. I saw her with her kids in social situations and noticed she was often the easy target for manipulative feedback from her kids like, "That's not fair". One day at a social event, Emily heard me talking with some other parents about guilt-free parenting. The next day, Emily made an appointment. She had one question: "What does guilt-free look like?" I asked for a little more clarity and the conversation went something like this:

> **Emily**: "Well when I have a rule, like, screen time ends at 7 pm; when we get to 7 pm and I say it's time, they say that it's not fair… they're in the middle of something… they want more time… and it turns into this big thing…. I end up feeling guilty no matter what I do. I have no idea how to make it fair."
>
> **Me**: "It's not your job to make everything fair. It's your job to raise accountable kids."

Emily: "But when the kids are telling me it's not fair, what can I do?"

Me: "Stop talking."

Emily: Confused silence…

Me: "You are allowing your kids to hold you as an emotional hostage."

Going back to your original question: "What does guilt-free look like?"

"It looks like logic, not emotion. When your kids are telling you it's not fair, they are playing on your emotions. The fact is, your rule is screen time ends at 7 pm. As the parent, you created a rule, therefore, it's a fact to your children. Treat it like one. You are allowing yourself to be emotionally manipulated into not following through. Plus, your lack of enforcing your rule is reinforcing their behavior. They know if they make you feel guilty, the likelihood is that you'll cave and they'll get what they want. Kids are way more perceptive than most parents give them credit for."

Emily: "Wow…"

Me: "You have to take non-negotiable action. Create boundaries without apology. Guilt emerges when there are inconsistencies between how you feel vs how you act. Choose to act on logic, not your feelings or your child's feelings."

Emily: "What a clear way to look at it."

Me: "Start with that one rule. Screen time ends at 7 pm. Repeat it, simply, early in the evening. And when 7 pm comes around, screens off. Anticipate the meltdown...they will react. You don't need to. You are coming from fact. They are coming from emotion. Don't join them."

The good news is, it worked. Emily stuck by this strategy with zero regret: after only three times it became fully effective. Once her kids realized she set a rule and unwaveringly enforced it, her kids learned she meant business and could not be taken emotional hostage with their whiny pleas. Emily came back for a few refresher sessions to help her over humps whenever she reverted to letting guilt creep in, but her success has been visible. The kids no longer run the show and their behavior has improved across the board.

Guilt Self-Reflections

1. Do you tell yourself that you can't do it all and then go ahead and try anyway?
2. What kind of guilt do you place on yourself?
3. Do you feel guilty for the way things are?
4. Do you feel guilty for things you've done or said?
5. Do you feel guilty for things your child has to deal with? Remember what's done is done. Let yourself off the hook and move on and teach your child to do the same.
6. What kind of guilt do you place on your child?
7. What kind of guilt do you let your kids place on you?
8. What kind of societal guilt do you take on?

Guilt Gamechangers

1. Think of ways you place too high of a standard on yourself. It sets you up to feel bad about not meeting unrealistic expectations. Accept yourself, as is.
2. Notice where you make emotional decisions. Practice swapping emotion for logic.
3. Ask yourself when you tend to feel most guilty, under what circumstances, and then be on high alert during those times.
4. Prioritize yourself. Make yourself the promise to never feel regret. Regret is fixable with an apology or clarification.

Takeaway Tool

Allowing yourself to feel guilt changes nothing!

Chapter 4

Are You for Sale?

"A friend to all is a friend to none."
~ Aristotle

Asking, "Are You for Sale?" is my euphemistic way of asking whether any pleading, whining, or negotiating gets you to change your established rules. Does that kind of behavior get you to compromise what you stand for? Know your values, know your rules, make them simple and clear, and stick to them under all circumstances. Don't keep your values and morals a secret. Tell your kids your bottom line every chance you get and live that bottom line loud and proud. That way, you'll have two legs to stand on when you say no.

As parents, we need to have our yesses and nos figured out ahead of time so our kids have clear boundaries they can easily understand. Know the principles that define you, and have them front and center so your child can see the character you embody.

My kids knew from a very young age their mom did not have a price for which she would sell out her principles or fall for bullshit. I knew I'd arrived when Matt's pre-teen friend—whose parents were for sale at bargain basement prices—tried to negotiate with me, like he did with his parents, for a later curfew. Matt chuckled and said, "Dude, it's not going to work, she doesn't fall for that!"

When we allow for bargaining, we give the impression that our rules are open to negotiation. Some kids have their parents well trained. They know just how to turn that no into a yes. There are parents who strive to be pleasers, who want their kids to like them, who want to be the cool parent or who want to avoid uncomfortable conflict. Selling your principles out to be the cool parent is just a bid for positive attention from your child. Having a need for that attention deeply diminishes your parental clout.

Say you've told your child growing up that he won't get a new car when he gets his license. Fast forward to high school. All your child's friends receive shiny, brand new cars at sixteen and your son begs you for a new set of wheels, despite what you've told him for years. Do you feel compelled to cave in to the pressure and follow the parental crowd to get Junior a new car? If your bottom line can be that easily compromised, your child will know that he can't depend on you to stand your ground in the face of pressure. Your compromising gives him tacit approval to blur his own bottom line and follow the crowd as he's watched you do.

When the time came for us, we made the decision to get our kids used, reasonably running manual cars. That way they had to focus on driving. We bought ourselves a few extra months of no texting and driving until they became more comfortable driving while multitasking (I'm not a proponent of texting and driving, I am just a realist, it will likely happen. Good thing I already learned to let go of control.) Of course, they wanted new cars like their friends but how's it feel to want?

Having Integrity Builds Integrity

Not being for sale is a great way to show our children we have integrity. Kids respond well when rules are clearly communicated and consistently enforced. Knowing what is expected of them and having those expectations consistently enforced helps kids feel successful and safe.

It's easier for kids to follow rules that are reliably carried out. A child craves security and safety from his parent. Even if the answer isn't what he wanted to hear, he needs to know he can count on his parent to do the right thing, every time. Steady, dependable direction from us is the building block to the structural integrity of our family.

Your Principles Help Build Theirs

Another benefit of not being for sale is it teaches kids values. It seems many people have a price if the payout is high enough. Capitulation or surrendering your principles may yield a temporary feeling of status, popularity, or power, but in the end you're left empty-handed because you stand for nothing.

A child learns to be firm in her principles by watching how her parents honor their principles. A child is more apt to say no to drugs, sex, peer pressure, and bullies if she's observed her parent not sell out when given the chance. It's important that a child knows her parents' boundaries are not open to compromise. Standing your ground and having established rules teaches values and creates life skills. Some of my favorites are hard work, altruism, gratitude, honesty, and loyalty.

Remember to Keep Your Ego Out of It

If you are willing to accept that your lack of consistency is what makes your kid argue with you and push the boundaries then you are on your way to not being for sale. Believe me, I know it's tempting to say yes to make your child happy. It feels so much better for us in the short run. It's hard walking on egg-shells when they hate you, towing the line, enforcing rules. It's not fun being the adult. Life is so much easier when there is no drama. However, compromising yourself for temporary harmony damages your child's future life skills as an adult. Temporary relief in those moments creates long-term coping problems for the child. Children need to know how it feels to hear "no," the answer they were already expecting to hear and are secretly grateful you didn't change.

Standing Up For Your Beliefs

1. Do you have the courage to choose a side, even if others disagree?
2. Will you stand up for other people who feel the same way that you do, even if it's not the popular position?
3. Think about how your child benefits from you standing by your beliefs, even if it creates temporary friction with her because she doesn't quite understand your position yet.

Your Behavior Is Contagious

Bad behavior is contagious: if you smoke, drink, cheat, lie, eat poorly, avoid exercise, or go to bed at an ungodly hour, yet you preach that your child should live an exemplary life, that's sell out behavior.

You've got to practice what you preach, maybe even to the extreme. Our children view us in black and white when they are young. There is no gray area for them. If they perceive us as selling out in any way or being inconsistent, it's hugely disappointing to them. My husband and I did our best to model those values daily. At least, I thought I modeled values and rocked my discipline, but I am human after all.

A not so funny story: While our kids are young, we tell them drinking is bad, drugs are bad, things are either good or bad. They understand absolutes, until, they don't. I'm not much of a drinker, but once a year when we trim the Christmas tree, it's been my tradition to have Baileys on ice while holiday decorating. When the kids were old enough to understand that Mom had alcohol in her cup, my ten-year old daughter barked at me, "There goes my role model for not drinking!" She could not have been more serious. One drink, one time a year and I was held to a ridiculous standard. It opened my eyes to witness how much kids take in everything we do. If we, as parents, so much as waffle, hesitate or have a weak moment, our kids stand ready to be the overseers of all our inconsistencies.

When we act inconsistently it confuses our kids. I'm glad my daughter felt comfortable stating her feelings. It gave me a window to learn and see our contradictions cause confusion when it comes to teaching our kids values. Our hypocrisy registers with them and my daughter taught me that with her angry observation. Mind you, it didn't change my behavior. I still treated myself with a drink when I wanted to. Her outburst showed me she was ready to learn about nuances. Life isn't black and white (drinking = bad; no drinking = good). Instead of taking her anger personally, it gave me an opportunity for a teachable moment.

Your child may not always hear your words but she does always see your actions. Actions get embedded on a subconscious level. What you do is way more memorable than what you say. Your child watches you at every turn, seeing how you respond and noticing how you handle situations. So, determine what you stand for, tell your child your limit, and stick to it. In other words: don't be for sale.

PS: *Our magic formula is to have very few rules, but enforce the few we have 100% of the time.*

Clear and consistent, time after time. If it isn't hard for us as parents; it isn't effective!

No Negotiating – No Means No

Teen: "Mom, all my friends are going to a concert tonight. Can I go?"

Mom: "No, you can't go, it's a school night."

Teen: "But Mom, I will get all my work done early, I have a ride there and back."

Mom: "Sorry. I said no."

Teen: "But Mom, please. I'm the only one of my friends not going, I'll get up on time for school the next day."

Mom gives thought to this and decides that her years' long rule of not going out on a school night is now up for debate. Mom doesn't want her daughter to be the only girl not going. That makes her look mean and her daughter is going to be mad at her for days which is uncomfortable. Mom changes her mind.

Mom: "All right, you can go, but don't go anywhere after the concert."

In this example, mom caved as her need to please her daughter overrode her initial answer. She was for sale. Mom undermined so many valuable lessons by waffling. First, her rules are no longer considered firm. All rules are now open to argument. She also prevented her daughter from experiencing disappointment. By mitigating her daughter's disappointment, she taught her negotiation, whining, or anguish are tactics she can use with teachers, bosses, or friends whenever authority gives her an answer she doesn't like. In essence, her daughter is being given a false sense of power. Inevitably, her daughter will make even more demands, increase the stakes on staying out later, not help out around the house, or barter over any other rule she doesn't like. None of us want to deal with a child who turns into an adult who behaves like that.

Be Dependable and Credible

It's late after sports practice. A pre-teen is waiting for his Dad. He texts,

"When will you be here to pick me up?"

If dad is twenty minutes away, he shouldn't text back, "Be there in a few minutes." Be honest. Inconsistency dilutes your dependability. If you tell your child you will be somewhere, be there or tell him the truth if you get delayed.

If you make plans with your child or say you will do something for him, stick to it. Don't assume he will forget or doesn't care. Follow through. He notices.

Clarity and Consistency = Trust and Respect

In a personal experience similar to the concert example above, I discovered that not being for sale can also be used preemptively. This works because the groundwork has been laid ahead of time. Clarity and consistency have been established. My kids know that my rules are not up for debate and my credibility is a given.

One of our triplets wanted to go to a weekday concert in high school and he texted me at lunch with all his friends gathered around. He knew I'd have some sassy response, but most of all, he knew he wasn't going. "Mom, can I go with the guys to see (insert rapper name here) on Wednesday night?"

As predicted, my answer was, "Are you smoking crack? It's a school night. Not going to happen."

In this case, he didn't want to go to the concert with these guys and he depended on me to enforce the rules so he'd have an excuse to say no!

I suspected that was the case because our kids knew better than to publicly call me out on my rules. He came home relieved I gave the answer he knew I would give. Our kids were told early on that they could always blame me or Dad when they didn't want to follow the crowd, or attend the sleepover, or go to the party. "Sorry, my Mom's a huge beeeatch, I can't go!" That was always fine by me. I had zero need for any of our kids' friends to like me. Their friends trusted me, respected me, and were a little afraid of me. As those friends got older, they loved hanging out at our house because they knew there were boundaries and they felt safe.

CASE STUDY – For Sale

Mom: Ruth. 1 Daughter, 6; 1 Son, 4 months

Ruth is a hardworking, slightly overwhelmed young mom with a 6-year old daughter named Stella and a 4-month old son, Noah. Ruth reached out to me because she was having a hard time sticking to "no" with Stella.

Stella's most troubling behavior occurred in public, specifically at the grocery store. She picked something off the shelf, often candy in the checkout line, demanded to have it, and threw a public fit if Mom said no. With Noah in hand, a cart full of groceries, places to get to, and disapproving customers lined up behind her, Ruth often wound up giving in. She described feeling so embarrassed by what other people might think of her, or of Stella, that she did whatever she needed to do to stop the screaming in that moment.

We worked together to practice flexing her "not for sale" muscle. I had her plan a store trip just for the purpose of retraining Stella. She reinforced expectations ahead of time, telling Stella they had to make a trip to the store and she would buy only what was on her list, nothing else. She took Stella to the store and shopped around for a bit, before deliberately turning into the candy aisle. Sure enough, Stella grabbed her favorite candy from the shelf and threw it into the cart. When Ruth took it back out, Stella began to whine. When Ruth did not respond, Stella tried to up her game. She threw a fit and screamed that she was starving, and accused her mom of never buying her anything

But Ruth was ready. She didn't pay attention to other people in the store. Ruth kept cool, focusing on her actions matching her words. She calmly left her entire cart and took Stella out of the store. When they got into the car, Ruth explained to Stella that she respected her right to be upset, but her method of expressing it was inappropriate. She also explained Stella must respect her mom's right to say no and mean it. Ruth allowed no more discussion on the matter. She let her few decisive words and actions do all the talking.

Once Ruth began having expectations and trained her daughter in behaving according to those expectations, Stella knew what was expected, or there would be consequences. Ruth realized when she allowed herself to be "for sale," Stella floundered and tested the limits uncomfortably.

Not Being for Sale Self-Reflections

1. Do you always practice what you preach?
2. How would you respond if you were called out by your child on accidental or intentional hypocrisy?
3. What are the subjects or situations where you have given into your child? Do you do this at the expense of your own rules?
4. On a scale of 1-10, with 10 being perfect, how consistent are you?

Not Being For Sale Gamechangers

1. Write down a list of your top 5 values. How consistently do you model them?
2. Are your values clearly communicated to your kids?
3. Write down a list of your top 5 rules. How consistently do you enforce them?
4. Do you feel pressure to capitulate based on what other parents are doing?

Takeaway Tool

When your words match your actions,
you are not for sale.

Chapter 5

Do You Have a System That Works?

"My bed is a magical place where I suddenly remember everything I was supposed to do."
~ Anonymous

When random strangers saw me out with all the kids, they inevitably asked, "How do you do it?" My answer was always, "I have a system for everything." When I use the word system, I'm not referring to a Susie homemaker, ultra-organized type household, although organization is part of it. In creating systems, the word system is a broader umbrella term that covers learning how to make your best decisions, organizing daily tasks, providing space for inspiration, and forming habits that create discipline.

Having a system for running your household provides a framework that quickly allows you to categorize items and find more efficient ways to customize how you handle daily tasks. Everything you do should have a purpose. Efficient systems bring structure and logical order to your home. Having a well-run home benefits everyone and helps us stay calm during the daily grind. Creating systems also helps you know when it's time to rotate your schedule if what you are currently doing no longer serves you. As you move through every phase of raising kids, at any time, you can reimagine your household whenever you need an updated routine. The goal is always to work smarter, not harder.

The Dynamic Decision Process™

In this chapter, I explore ideas on how to turn your home into a well-oiled machine. You want to have existing systems that are easy for others to implement. Whatever system you create needs to be conceptualized first and that creation falls on you, the parent. Once in place, the family can easily see what is expected. Having a system elicits a nonverbal expectation of where things go and how things go.

When parents asked me how I managed to run a family of six, a sales business, be a wife, and also find time to mentor other parents, I was challenged to reflect on my own practices so I could add value to my answer. I found I organize my thoughts and make decisions in a unique way. The technique I intrinsically use has served me well in life and in business.

I define this technique as The Dynamic Decision Process. DDP is the ability to make optimal decisions quickly in a changing environment. You do this by dynamically shifting your thinking from short-term to long-term then back to short-term all within a moment or two. It's the capacity to visualize the situation you are in in that moment (short term), transition to the big picture (long-term) in that same moment, to run that situation through a bigger, long-term perspective so you can come up with your most fully considered solution. This decision-making process simplifies and streamlines the barrage of chaos that occurs on a daily basis with having a family. Best of all, using the DDP saves precious time because our decisions will be well-informed the first time. There is no repeating or do-overs of the same task when you determine the best, most-efficient way to tackle it the first time.

The Dynamic Decision Process adeptly combines thinking in two directions, short-term and long-term, one after the other. Speed is paramount. Doing this will keep you out of the weeds and will allow you to think more globally to help run your hectic days seamlessly. Most people are either stuck in the big picture or stuck in the minutiae. Toggling between the two fluidly helps you prioritize your actions and come up with better ways of doing daily tasks.

Another way to think of The Dynamic Decision Process is this: short term/details = analytical thought; long-term/big picture = practical thought. Blend the two for dynamic decision-making. You don't want to be just a micro thinker or just a macro thinker. You can teach yourself to do both, within any given circumstance, to achieve the best possible outcome every time.

Our brain is wired to see situations in the short-term. We aren't as good at seeing long-term. With awareness, we can train ourselves to be good at both. It takes practice. The Dynamic Decision Process is like flexing a muscle in your mind. With repetition, it becomes easier to alternate between both short-term and long-term thinking the more you do it.

Cultivating a big picture view, in any circumstance, prevents us from spinning our wheels in the monotony of routine. Big picture thinking people are comfortable with diverse ideas, opposing thought, and with uncertainty in general. However, if we are mired in the minutiae, not able to see the big picture, we end up expending energy on the wrong matters, duplicating time and effort, feeling exhausted, and not understanding why.

Drilling down on only details leaves us feeling busy but unproductive. Therefore, we want to use big picture thinking to assist with our short-term decisions.

Organizing Your Thoughts With DDP

When daily non-essentials start to become stressful, ask yourself why you're upset and what's causing you the most work. Take your short-term struggles and shift up to the big picture thinking to figure out how to prioritize your next move from the macro view. The big picture view will help you determine (1) is this even important, (2) will it resolve on its own, and (3) if this needs my attention is there another or better way to handle it.

EXAMPLE #1

On a particular evening, you make everyone's favorite glop casserole dinner. Your child needs help with algebra homework, you had a big disagreement earlier with a friend over continually cancelled plans, and your dog just threw up on the carpet. Multiple situations happening simultaneously all need your attention and you feel overwhelmed because, let's be honest, every minute of every day is like this with kids. Instead of allowing the moments to accumulate to where you feel overwhelmed, use the DDP. Your brain will react like this: short term = child can try to figure out homework himself first; big picture = set a specific time with your child each night just for homework help. You will be available at that specific time, and your child can plan homework help accordingly. Shifting up to the big picture allows you to come up with an idea that eliminates this panicked homework request every night.

Short-term = dog vomit needs attention now; big picture = what did the dog get into, does his food need to be changed, should I take him to the vet or put him in a contained pen in the kitchen to wait this out? Shifting up to the big picture allows you to consider the potential other reasons the dog may be sick which eliminates more vomit episodes.

Short-term = make dinner; big picture = I'm tired, should we do take out or go out to give myself a break tonight. Shifting up to the big picture allows you to consider taking a break from the nightly cooking chore.

Short-term = connect with my friend and resolve our disagreement; big picture = does this friendship still serve us both, do I fight with this friend a lot, what was my part of this fight, what was her part and do I want this friendship long-term or do I not need to resolve this any time soon? Shifting up to the big picture allows you to consider whether your minimal free time is worth surrounding yourself with a friendship that may or may not be productive to your well-being.

Using The Dynamic Decision Process helps you come up with more thoroughly thought-out methods that eliminate daily repetitive issues. Those are the issues that stack up and contribute to your ongoing stress. It forces you to consider your situation from every angle so a system can be put into place that alleviates that ongoing stress.

EXAMPLE #2

Every day, multiple times a day, you forget where you put your keys. You spend at least five minutes before leaving the house each time searching for them. Using The Dynamic Decision Process, you can resolve it this way: short-term = retrace your steps when you came through the door; big picture = ask yourself how you can avoid this in the future. Have one location dedicated to keys, wallet, and phone with a specific shelf in a convenient room. Shifting up to the big picture allows you to analyze this recurring stressor from macro mode which challenges you to come up with an idea that solves a daily, time-wasting problem.

This energetic exchange in your brain can take place with every aggravating problem. Toys left in the family room, coats left in the entryway, kids tugging on your leg for attention, nighttime routines gone awry. Don't let the irritation of the moment get the best of you. There is a creative, big picture way to solve anything. Just stop in the moment and challenge yourself to consider if there is a way to make one big decision to stop the need for repetitive little ones. Once you have a system for organizing your thoughts, an easier daytime routine begins to fall into place.

P.S. *Here's a fun trick: When you truly can't decide between two choices, flip a coin. While it's in the air, you will quickly realize which choice you are hoping for.*

Organizing Daily Tasks

Organization allows your home to be more well-run and well-run translates to breezier days for you. One of the easiest ways I found to keep myself organized was to have daily tasks that kept the heart of our home beating. I've isolated the key areas where I invested effort into daily tasks and found the most reward:

Create your shopping list, display it publicly, and everyone contributes. If it's not on the list, it doesn't get purchased (if you were the last one to finish the chips and didn't add it, you wait a week until I go shopping again. By the way, yes, I only shopped once a week to keep from cluttering my day-to-day since I ran my business from home all day. Who has time to shop three to four times a week?)

Sticky notes are the superstar of my success. If I think it, I write it down immediately and put the sticky note by my purse or my keyboard where I know I'll see it and have to act on it. I never set myself up for failure. I have a foolproof system in place for everything that doesn't let me down so I won't forget an idea that pops into my head.

Create your family calendar, display it publicly, and everyone contributes. I used my old-fashioned paper desktop At-a-Glance calendar and it has not failed me for 25+ years running. It contained everything for four athletic kids' practices, games, pick-up times, doctor appointments, meetings, plus all my and my husband's events. We were all responsible for keeping it up-to-date.

Get yourself ready in the morning first. For a baby or toddler, use a bouncer or playpen and take your shower, do your hair, and make her wait. If you are ready for the day first thing, you feel way more productive. When she is older, get up earlier or turn the lock on her door backwards so you can lock her in her room (until she is independent enough to be alone). She waits until you are ready to go and all else falls into place. Don't convince yourself you can't shower or get ready with a baby. It's possible, even with four.

Arrange to run errands alone. Running errands goes more quickly and with less stress if you can count on someone to watch the kids for a few hours a week. I came up with two ideas that served me incredibly well. One, contact a local senior living apartment and ask the manager to post a notice for childcare help two to three days a week for a few hours. An older, independent grandma would love to share her wealth of experience with you and she will likely be quite trustworthy. Two, most churches offer a free employment website where you can list your job, hours, needs, and get contacted by someone interested in helping. Both these options are inexpensive and they allow you time to run errands kid-free.

Inspiration – Creative Use of Space

Creative Use of Space is really just making imaginative use of your existing space. Here's how I evaluated space: I made it work for me so our four kids could be inspired in their own home and have their own sliver of space to do it. When the kids were young I became obsessed with reading remodel magazines at Home Depot because it got my creative juices flowing, even if I couldn't afford my own remodel.

After getting ideas, I looked at my home through fresh eyes. Having a traditional dining room was an abandoned traditional space for us. For some people, that room is their living room. So, we turned our dining room into a huge playpen when the triplets were ages one to three. You don't have to have triplets to do this! I bought an outdoor adjustable, folding plastic dog gate and connected it into a large round circle. Then, I bought three to four flat sheets and sewed them together, tied them to the outside of the gate and voila, a safe, roomy playpen that protected the carpet from vomit or leaky diapers. We threw the kids and the toys in there and went about our business. Our older son climbed in and out to play when he wanted. It was convenient and safe and the best use of a room I didn't need to use daily.

After the kids outgrew the playpen, I fashioned a "pop up" learning center in the dining room. I bought a cheap little shelf with bins and a used school table with chairs. It was like a mini school room. I filled the bins with various mind-engaging activities (crafts, coloring, drawing books, etc.) Use anything your child shows interest in building, creating, or designing. I visited school supply stores to get ideas and then rotated the bin contents. To say the kids loved that space is an understatement. I still have artwork and ironed bead hearts displayed from those days on my office bulletin board. There may be some other unused corner in your home where you can put a portable table, waterproof tablecloth, and a tiny chair for creative activities. Even the smallest studio apartment has a corner space that can be reconceptualized to give your child his own little slice of freedom.

This concept still has merit even when the kids get older. When our oldest was ten to twelve years old, he showed an interest in building model airplanes. We bought an inexpensive, folding puzzle table and found a spot for it near our kitchen table. He owned this space. The table was all his to spread out his glue, model pieces, and paper instructions where it remained untouched. I paid no mind to this table in the corner of our kitchen. I didn't care if a neighbor stopped by and saw this messy table in the middle of our kitchen. I prioritized our cherished space for the kids with no concern as to how it might make the house look.

Our son sat for hours creating and building and I didn't care that "his" table had glue and paint all over it. Another unexpected benefit to this idea turned out to be his space was in the center of our home where he could still be part of all the goings on while simultaneously doing his own thing. As an adult now, he still proudly displays the model airplanes he built. He has gone on to get his private pilot's license and plans to make a career in the Air Force. The table only stayed in our kitchen for about a year, just a phase, but was critical to his future.

Discipline - Forming Daily Habits

The last aspect to creating systems is forming daily habits. Habits develop into a comforting action that becomes the heartbeat of your home. Having regular habits forms a routine. A routine creates a sense of order for the family. That familiar order and routine offers one more way for kids to feel independent. Habits are similar to traditions. Kids thrive on both and they get their sense of family and belonging from those rituals.

By forming daily habits, your child comes to depend on you. She experiences how disciplined habit patterns help her home feel like a safe and secure place to exist. Forming daily habits gives your child a sense of normalcy, something she can depend on. That sense of normalcy translates to relieving stresses from the outside world. In her home, she grows to count on her consistent routine and daily habits.

How do you want to build your daily habits so they suit you and your family? Your habits will change as your child grows and as he understands the reasoning behind daily habits. Having daily habits is one of the easiest ways to instill self-discipline into your child.

Whether it's flossing your teeth daily or exercising or limiting dessert to three nights a week, whatever habits you deem important, they will show your child there are things we need to do first before we enjoy fun time. When I became a full-fledged adult, completely living on my own for the first time, I felt buried under all the responsibilities that now fell solely on me to handle. I had to remember to pay the rent on time, take my vitamins, clean the house, make doctor appointments for myself, and get my oil changed. I believe I transitioned to being a successful young adult because of the habits my mom established, habits I carried with me into adulthood. Important things needed to be done first; paying the rent before treating myself to a shopping spree at the mall, grocery shopping for food before partying all weekend with my friends.

Being able to fall back on daily habits allows your child to not feel overwhelmed by life when it gets complicated. Daily habits keep us on track in life. They keep us organized and they give us discipline.

System Self-Reflections

1. Focus on conquering the moment you are in. When you examine the moment by applying the big picture to it, you will find ways to improve every situation in your life.
2. Look at your home life through a more consciously aware lens to stay a step ahead of stress and you won't get bogged down in mindless reactions.
3. Write a household goal, then answer why that is a goal for you. Apply a system to it.

System Gamechangers

1. Visualize your ideal for how you want your household to look, run, and feel. Write down everything you notice about your ideal household including sites, smells, sounds and colors.
2. Notice how you feel in this ideal household.
3. Make a list of ways you can prioritize creative use of space in your own home.
4. Make a list of the top five habits most important to you.

Takeaway Tool

Micro thinking + Macro thinking =
Best possible outcome every time.

Chapter 6

The Parenting Superpower We All Have

"One choice can transform you. One choice can destroy you. One choice will define you."
~ Veronica Roth

One of the most influential books I ever read was *Your Greatest Power,* written by J. Martin Kohe (Napoleon Hill Foundation, 1953.) It's a small, unassuming book packed with practical advice about the greatest power we all possess. I read it in my early twenties and it rattled my brain. *Your Greatest Power* energized me to start my own business, pick a different roommate, and buy my own car. I didn't realize my potential worth financially, until I read it.

After negotiating with a potential new boss, who didn't want to pay me for what I knew I could deliver, I decided to do it for myself. I've never looked back.

Those monumental changes took place in my life after being reminded of the power that already exists in me, and in all of us. Fast forward, thirty plus years later, and I'm still so hyped about this concept I'm upgrading this greatest power to our greatest Superpower! This Superpower, when observed, is the key to your happiness and it will immediately instill accountability, perspective, and enjoyment into your life. Best of all, this Superpower doesn't require any special educational degrees or expensive props and we all have access to it. Even better, it's free. All that is needed is your awareness of it and your discipline to use it.

Your Superpower is your freedom and ability to choose.

You are able, at any time, to exercise your free will and make your own choices to select your own thoughts. Your ability to choose has always been, and will always be, your greatest Superpower. You can choose to go or not go, you can choose to say it or not say it, you can choose how you hear or interpret words, you can choose your outlook in every situation. You can choose to free yourself, to inspire yourself, to change yourself, or to embrace yourself.

Choice is the key. The freedom and ability to choose is the secret to being a happy person. Somehow, sadly, most of us forget we always have the power to actively choose whatever thoughts and actions our heart desires. Our ability to choose is the most consequential and significant resource in our lives.

Using Our Superpower as an Adult

As adults, we face making hundreds, thousands, millions of choices every day. We may not always realize it, but every second of our waking moments provides an opportunity for us to choose what we think and how we want to react. Take a moment to truly reconnect with this readily available, powerful gift. No one but you is in charge of your thoughts or your choices. Isn't that empowering? When you don't like something, just choose something else. It's your right. You never have to let a circumstance dictate your story.

Everything in your life happens from your choices. Your job, your friends, your relationships, and your attitude all exist in their current state as a result of your ability to choose. If you think you have no control over the outcome of a situation, all you have to do is backtrack any upsetting or positive occurrence until you expose your original choice that led you to your current situation. If you are honest with yourself, you will see the connection between a choice you made and the outcome of that choice. Maybe the current outcome wasn't your hope or intention, but that doesn't erase the fact your executed choice led to that outcome—good or bad.

I have had to remind myself of this gift many times. When I'm in a rut or feeling especially stressed from balancing everyone else's needs over my own, I activate my own power. I'll choose to work out or go to bed earlier or expect less of myself or let things go, like the cleaning or cooking. "Kids, we're going out for dinner tonight!" If I feel pissed, I may choose to give it time, get more information, eat chocolate, or swear my ass off! If I'm happy, I may choose to savor that moment, tell someone something positive, wallow in gratitude, or eat chocolate.

We never have to settle for any condition in our lives. We all have the ability to change any condition by changing the way we view that condition. Our actions and our thoughts are all up to us. Isn't that motivating?

Recently, the computer that I run my business from needed repair. Without access to it, my business stands still. The news kept getting worse as to how long I'd be without it. Since I exhausted all options within my control, I channeled my thoughts into all the other tasks I put aside and could now finish without my computer luring me away. I finished reading the two books I started. I took some much needed downtime. I reconnected with friends. I cleared up piles of projects I hadn't finished or had been avoiding. Instead of staying in anger and frustration, I wound up being proud of myself for all I decided to accomplish! And, I ate chocolate! We all have those choices. There is always a new way to view every situation.

P.S. *It's important to note that we never want to use our power of choice to blame others. It's weak-minded. We can always find some way we've participated in the situation. Even if it means that our participation was to do nothing or not respond. And we have always made a decision, conscious or not, to feel a certain way about it. The way we feel is never somebody else's doing.*

Using Our Superpower as a Parent

As a parent, our choices affect the whole family. If our job is miserable, or takes us from home too long or our partner isn't carrying their weight, we have the ability to choose different courses of action for better outcomes that help our family.

Whenever I've felt stuck or restricted by my parenting responsibilities, I remind myself that I have the lone ability to choose to view the situation in a variety of ways other than how I currently view it. We can make the choice to engage, to overlook, to be patient, to argue, or to forgive. These actions are all within our control when it comes to our kids.

Our Kids Have This Superpower, Too!

As we revel in how liberating our Superpower makes us feel as adults, hold that thought and apply it to your child. What easier way to create independence, confidence, and consequence than by letting your child practice using her Superpower whenever possible?

As adults, if we don't show up for work, we lose our job. As parents, we want to recreate that realistic societal framework in our homes so our children are free to learn consequences to their choices every day, without judgment or punishment.

Say your teenage son, flush with money from his first-ever paycheck, wants to spend it all on a fly-fishing rod. It's his money, his choice. However, there will be consequences to his decision. If he decides to spend all his money, your job will be to mirror any life consequence that transpires. There will be no money left for gas, dates, or food. He waits until he earns his next paycheck. This takes discipline on your part not to get involved and solve it or lend him money. You respect him enough to let him figure it out.

What if your child decides she doesn't want to wear her coat to school on a frigid day? Who will be cold, you or her? Why court a fight? Life's consequence will intervene. When you deny your child's right to learn her own way, you prevent her from using her own creative methods to experience lessons, which delays growth. Each child has a need to control and direct her own thoughts and choices for optimum understanding and development. All of this can effectively be accomplished by offering choices. Doing this gets her closer to understanding her own Superpower.

Give Them Choices About Their Choices

Life is a series of choice and consequence. As parents, we can reflect the same choice and consequence conditions in our homes that our kids will deal with in the real world. Our home provides a safe place for our children to experiment with decisions.

To do this, give your child the opportunity to take full responsibility for his choices and not have circumstances dictate his story. Give him the chance to discover self-generated choices without your input. It starts with something as simple as creating his morning routine: brush his teeth first or his hair? Sleep with the stuffed fox or the teddy bear? Cereal or toast for breakfast? Then you give larger windows of time for choices: clean the playroom now or in an hour? Then set the timer. Mow the lawn on Saturday or Sunday? Then help him follow-through. Every chance you get, on inconsequential events, say, "you choose."

When our kids were teenagers, we would say on a Friday, "It's your turn to vacuum. Please get it done by Sunday." They knew what was expected of them and could use their own timeline to get it done but we set the deadline. Helping our children get in touch with their own Superpower pays huge dividends toward their self-confidence.

Don't Offer a Choice You Don't Want Them to Take

All kids test the limits. But we want to avoid giving a response that is heard as a threat or ultimatum. Sometimes we speak before we think and unintentionally make a statement, through frustration, that gives our kids a choice we don't want them to take.

Next time you are about to state an ultimatum, where your child could argue back "or what" - stop - and sidestep the inevitable power struggle you are leading you both into. You have the skills to predict when you are about to back yourself or your child into a corner. The way to avoid most fights is to not draw a hard line, for yourself or your child. The key to good communication with your kids is making non-directive, broad stroke statements that keep their own choices alive.

I've seen this scenario more than once: a child chooses not to do their homework, not study, or they come home past curfew and in response the parents take their car keys. When we threaten our child with taking keys to get him to follow our rules, what we are really doing is limiting our own choices, too. Does he walk to school, or do we get disrupted by having to drive him, or do other people have to be inconvenienced to accomplish our goal. Do you really want to play Driving Miss Daisy with your kid?

As the dominoes fall, what's our back-up plan? What's our threat *really* trying to control? What we've done is box ourselves into a corner. We heard the words come out of our mouths, and now we're stuck. We are in a never-ending loop of trying to set boundaries.

Our son Scott had a friend whose parents were known for setting these types of conditions. The problem was, when they took his keys for two weeks, it was our son who ended up driving him to school every day and then home from practice. What if he hadn't chosen to step in? Were those parents prepared to have their son be truant or walk three miles to school there and back? Would they have missed work to drive him to and from school each day?

Clearly, they had not considered their threat might lead to bigger problems for them or might inconvenience those around them. They didn't consider how the dominoes would fall if someone like Scott hadn't stepped in for the good of the team and his friend. In reality, the taking of the keys didn't really restrict their son that much, he just got chauffeured by my son instead of driving himself. Big deal! Much more on what you *can* do instead of taking keys in Chapter 14.

Bottom line: Don't lay out conditions you can't or won't back up. These situations will show up more often than you think. Every rule you set has a potential "or else" embedded in it. And it's really important to catch on right now to the fact that threats and ultimatums are not deterrents, they are obstacles. They are obstacles that your child may choose to go around, over, or through. Are you prepared if they do?

For instance, suppose you promise to take away a fun activity the whole family enjoys if your child talks back to you. You might regret cancelling a family outing or activity and disappointing everyone due to one person's choices. Or suppose you threaten to kick your child out of the house if he chooses to drink. Once faced with an episode of him drinking, are you going to stick to kicking him out of the house? And are you willing to deal with all the dominoes that will follow?

Superpower Self-Reflections

1. Do you blame your kids or others for your feelings of frustration or being overwhelmed?
2. Are you willing to give up control to let your kids make their own choices?
3. Are you in the habit of fixing things when your kids make poor choices?
4. Do you have more rules than you need?

Superpower Gamechangers

1. Start using any opportunity to say "you choose" to your child by allowing small daily choices for your child that are doable. Then graduate to more important, age-appropriate decisions. Remember to stay out of the choices you see that are not good (safety is the exception.) Allow life to teach your child the consequence of his choice.
2. Make a list of the situations or circumstances in which you feel frustration or being overwhelmed with your parenting.
3. Make a list of all the rules you can think of that you have set for your child.
    a. Cross out any rules that sprang up in the heat of a moment.
    b. List any ultimatums you hear yourself saying or have heard yourself say in response to one of the rules being broken.

Takeaway Tool

I have the freedom and ability to choose,
and so do they.

Chapter 7

The Magic Mantra... Repeat After Me

"You cannot control the behavior of others, but you can always choose how you respond to it."
~ Roy T. Bennett, The Light in the Heart

The Magic Mantra is a cumulation of the chapters in Part One, with their content boiled down into one simple soundbite. It's the Mother of All Secrets to Parenting Without Giving a F^ck and to improving every relationship in your life.

This mantra was born at the height of my most thankless and trying times: pre-adolescence and the teen years, times four. During the kids' lengthy transition from me being their Mommy, to me being their Mom, to me being their "What the hell do you know; you're so embarrassing" parental unit, this Magic Mantra saved the day and saved my sense of self.

At first, as parents, our children completely need us in every circumstance. Our participation in the early years is craved, celebrated, even solicited. Gradually, as our child ages, our involvement becomes annoying to him and, soon we find our engagement is often rejected, ignored, and even shunned by the time pre-teen years emerge. As our child grows, we need to pay attention to when our advice and attachment should start receding to match the level of our child's growth. During my detachment process, the Magic Mantra was born.

Now, Dear Reader, I bequeath this magical life saver to you. Your Magic Mantra is: *I'm Only in Charge of Me; I'm Not in Charge of You.*

These words, when thought, felt, and said, honestly and with a sense of release, form the very foundation of *Parenting Without Giving a F^ck.* The Magic Mantra sets aside your ego. It releases your need for controlling others. It alleviates feelings of guilt. It prevents you from being for sale. It's the perfect manifestation of being free to choose your own thoughts and actions. It's your ticket to being an independent thinker and to developing independent-minded, accountable kids. It magically liberates you from taking on anyone else's drama. The Magic Mantra is your get-out-of-drama-free card!

I'm Only in Charge of Me; I'm Not in Charge of You.

The Magic Mantra is the ultimate boundary setting tool. It's practical and it's easy to use. Memorize it now and never forget it. You have been given a secret tool that, when repeated to yourself, will fortify your personal boundaries with each challenge, stressful situation, mean word spoken, or bit of drama you allow yourself to get sucked into. *I'm Only in Charge of Me; I'm Not in Charge of You,* enhances the trust in ourselves that we've been building. We don't need to take responsibility for what others do, say, or choose. We can give ourselves permission to de-clutter our lives from other people's choices. Starting right now. Give yourself the gift of being in charge of only you!

To lay the foundation for the Magic Mantra, it's helpful to remember there are things you can control—your goals, your effort, your willingness to learn from mistakes, your responses, your actions in general—and there are things you can't control—what others say or do, what others think, how others feel, the weather, the past, aging.

I'm Only in Charge of Me; I'm Not in Charge of You gives you instant perspective. It takes the pressure off all the decisions you think you need to make, whether those decisions are on behalf of your child or on behalf of any other person in your life. Repeating these words to yourself will force you to step back and assess your position on any situation. You can then decide if you are required to act or if the other person should act. Gradually you will find yourself reacting less, freeing yourself up to stress less.

Understanding the Magic Behind Your Mantra

There are many layers getting yourself to the point where you embrace *"I'm Only in Charge of Me; I'm Not in Charge of You."* First, it takes some readiness on your part to be in a place where you feel prepared to release others from your opinions and release yourself from needing to give your opinions. Second, believe this is what's best for you and for the other person. Take the leap of faith this mantra works, on many levels.

Magic Mantra Mentality

You let others take on their own responsibility and let others make their own choices.

You have zero ownership over anyone else's choices.

There are no feelings of spite or gloating. You are not thinking, "I'll be saying I told you so," or "You'll see I was right, sucker."

You are not mad.

You have no personal attachment to the other person's consequence from his choice.

You are neutralizing yourself by being in charge of yourself only. This empowers others to find their own solutions.

You are not manipulating or punishing. You feel true respect for the other person.

This mantra does not work when you are in a space of feeling ill-intentioned or vengeful. You must simply let go and take no ownership of other's decisions as well as no ownership of any outcome from someone else's actions, because you are only in charge of you!

How Using The Magic Mantra Works with Your Child

I'm Only in Charge of Me; I'm Not in Charge of You is like a bridge between our best parenting intentions and the best outcome for our child. We always start out thinking we are doing the right thing by getting involved or making decisions for our child, but ultimately, we shortchange him.

For the Magic Mantra to work most magically with your child, first establish and communicate your basic rules so they are clear. Within the parameters of your rules, *I'm Only in Charge of Me; I'm Not in Charge of You* will release you from yelling or needing time outs. You are only responsible for creating and communicating the rules. Children will know the consequence of not following the rules ahead of time because they will be the author of the consequence. More on that concept in Chapter 14.

Be firm about what you will do, not what you will make the child do:

Established rule: We leave at 7 AM for school.

I'm sorry your shoes aren't on. We leave at 7 AM shoes or not. *I'm only in charge of me, I'm not in charge of you.* She may miss the nature walk (like my daughter did) but you don't care; you are unbothered. She will have to explain why her shoes aren't on. You will only have to do this one, maybe two times at most. Our actions win over constant reminding, yelling, cajoling day after day.

Established rule: We clean up our mess; I only serve dinner on a clean kitchen table.

The table is a mess. No dinner is served until it's clean. *I'm only in charge of me, I'm not in charge of you.* They will be hungry but you are unaffected until the table is clean and then you serve dinner. You have rules and you mean business.

Established rule: Allocate time for homework each night.

His grades are bad and he can't play football. *I'm only in charge of me, I'm not in charge of you.* It is incredibly tempting to get involved here but this teaches him the result of not studying. He's in charge of himself and needs to figure out how to step up. You already graduated from high school and this doesn't involve you.

Established rule: Use your words; don't throw a tantrum.

Your daughter screams, throwing herself on the ground, behaving like a crazy person - *I'm only in charge of me, I'm not in charge of you.* I'm choosing to completely ignore her, leave the room, and act as if she isn't even in this dimension. What fun is throwing a tantrum without an audience? I don't get mad or give her behavior a side glance. She gets my attention when she calms herself down and uses her words.

Established rule: Get your driver's license at sixteen.

She refuses to get her license. She is either scared, feeling lazy or doesn't see the value. *I'm only in charge of me, I'm not in charge of you.* I respect your decision but I will not validate it by always being available to drive you everywhere. She can look into public transportation or having a friend drive her to school or to work. I may choose to drive her on occasion, but I will not allow the problems from her decision to become my problems.

It's Not Just for Kids!

Using this mantra became a turning point for me because *I'm Only in Charge of Me; I'm Not in Charge of You* became a successful component to all my relationships, including with my friends, husband, parents, and co-workers: not just my kids. Stress melted away as I stopped getting involved in problems that didn't concern me and that I didn't need to have control over. I relinquished control of what need not affect me and flourished where I could make the most impact in my own life.

A quick personal story illustrates my use of the Magic Mantra. My husband loves his job. Being a fighter pilot, it's easy to understand why, but he regularly worked fourteen to sixteen-hour days. He also loves his family, but if I remained quiet and OK at home, he contentedly allowed himself to put in long hours at work. I'd wait for him to get home so we could all eat together, take the kids to a movie, or the park. At first, I grew mad having to wait for him to get home and annoyed he put so much time in at the squadron.

One day, I decided *he chose* to work those hours and *I chose* to wait with frustration. From then on, I switched gears. I realized I am in charge of whether I wait past 5:30 p.m. or not. I am not in charge of the hours he chooses to work. It's me that is in charge of the schedule at home with the kids. I started eating when we were ready between 5:30-6:30 p.m. If he missed dinner, he could warm up leftovers. I took the kids to the movies or some other event and made memories with them that we enjoyed. This was not done with spite; it was done matter-of-factly. I communicated to him that I would no longer wait past 5:30 p.m. for him to come home if me and the kids wanted to eat or go out.

My choices did not come from a place of anger. That is the key to the Magic Mantra. I just acted in the capacity of making my own decisions based on what I had control over. He quickly decided he didn't want to miss out and it didn't take long for him to cut back to more regular hours to find his own balance. You can't force anyone to find his own balance. His behavior didn't change due to me whining, manipulating or being passive aggressive, or dropping truth bombs hoping he'd figure it out. There was no pressure, fighting or guilt-tripping, just quiet, independent action on my part. If he chose to continue working those hours, that was OK, too. That was his choice, but he couldn't have both. I'm only in charge of what I will do.

This mantra can get applied to literally every scenario in your life. You are not responsible for your parent's divorce, or for your friend's bad relationship. You are not responsible for the guilt your sibling tries to impose on you because she thinks Mom likes you best. Other people's thoughts and feelings are not within your control. Their thoughts contain their ego's feelings being projected onto you, if you let them. What are you in control of? You, and how you choose to respond to any given situation and what you choose to take on.

How Using Your Magic Mantra Works with Your Spouse, Parent, Friend, Sibling, Co-Worker

- It's too bad you don't like your restaurant dinner again – I like mine and *I'm only in charge of me, I'm not in charge of you.* (Each person solves their own likes and dislikes, don't make this my fight.)

- I go to practice every day so I get better, sorry you are not playing varsity – *I'm only in charge of me, I'm not in charge of you.* (Each person determines his own work ethic.)

- I'm sorry you drank too much and feel like crap all day – *I'm only in charge of me, I'm not in charge of you.* (I've mastered my own balance, you need to find yours.)

- I'm sorry you are held captive by your phone and get visibly angry when you read the news - *I'm only in charge of me, I'm not in charge of you.* (I've compartmentalized, tuned-out and found a productive use of my time that is more interesting for me.)

What Does the Magic Mantra Expose in You?

If you are having a resistance to the notion of *I'm Only in Charge of Me; I'm Not in Charge of You* in a particular situation, then that situation may be highlighting where you are challenged from one of the earlier chapters (ego, control, guilt, being for sale, no faith in your superpower.)

So, what does the Magic Mantra expose in you?

You justify getting involved by thinking, "I'm just trying to help." – *That's ego.*

You justify getting involved by thinking, "I'm going to make her see she's wrong, and I'm right." – *That's control.*

You justify getting involved by thinking, "If she doesn't listen to me, she'll regret it." – *That's guilt (you put onto others.)*

You justify getting involved by thinking, "If she does what I want now, I'll reward her with whatever she asks for later." – *That's being for sale.*

If you justify getting involved by thinking, "I just want them to make the right choice." – *That's not honoring our superpower or theirs.*

The essence of this mantra is in not allowing yourself to take on the consequences and stress of someone else's choices. It requires training yourself not to get involved in every exchange with your kids, your friends or family members. Most of the time when someone speaks to you, they only need you to listen. They don't always want or need your two cents.

Recall this old saying about advice: "Wise men don't need it and fools don't heed it." Never pass up the opportunity to shut the f^ck up. Man, have I had to remind myself of that more times than I can count. After offering up my very best unsolicited advice, I'd get angry or frustrated when my advice wasn't taken and the person ended up in the bad situation, as predicted. Control, anyone?

It wasn't until I had kids that I realized how presumptuous it was of me to think that I needed to solve someone else's problems. The only way to hold my kids accountable or truly help a friend, sibling, coworker, or my husband was to realize they don't always need me to solve their problems. In fact, their "problem" might not even be a problem for them. Who am I to say? I had to practice thinking this way, as you'd practice learning a foreign language: daily reminders to myself to butt out, until I came up with the handy Magic Mantra. Once committed to memory, magic commenced and my own home was filled with kids who felt more responsible with their choices and real-life, practical skills were developed daily. I also enjoyed an even better comradery with my husband and my friendships were so much more enjoyable with two-sided listening and exchanging of ideas, without me having a personal stake in the outcome.

When using the Magic Mantra as parents, we have to remind ourselves that kids are "adults in training" and they invariably will make decisions that we don't agree with. The trick to staying out of each tale of drama, deceit, or drivel is to remain unruffled, unaffected, and confident that they will figure it out, eventually. How can we best negotiate with a stubborn child, apathetic partner, or manipulative friend? *I'm Only in Charge of Me; I'm Not in Charge of You* - that's how!

One Last Unexpected Benefit - How Magic Mantra Taught Me Compassion & Forgiveness

Once I became adept at using the Magic Mantra, I noticed something else change inside me. I grew up a bit. I didn't get worked up over what other people thought, said, or did. It taught me how to stop holding grudges and how to let go of, or re-conceptualize, the other person's position. I was easily able to recognize the validity of someone else's perspective. Before the Magic Mantra, I was much more opinionated, less willing to see another person's point of view, and more apt to be judgmental. With the Magic Mantra, my stance on any given subject became cracked wide open. I could bring my opinion forward with confidence and let my opinion stand alone and release others from having to see my side while simultaneously becoming more receptive to other people's viewpoints and beliefs. I let the personal contest go.

Except for our kids' sporting events of course—make sure you never sit near me!

CASE STUDY – Magic Mantra

Mom: Carmen. 1 Daughter, 13; 1 Son, 6

When Carmen came to see me, her daughter Evie was 13 and in 8th grade. Carmen needed ways to talk to Evie about all the drama going on with friends at school. Evie fell into a very typical pattern of getting sucked into other people's stories. She often came home upset about drama that had nothing whatsoever to do with her. Evie grew increasingly anxious and depressed from it.

The final straw that brought Carmen to see me was when Evie talked about friends she'd known since kindergarten and how mean they were to her two of her new friends. Evie felt heartbroken with the way her old friends were turning on people. Carmen hadn't finished her story before I knew Evie would benefit greatly from embracing the Magic Mantra – *I'm Only in Charge of Me, I'm Not in Charge of You*. Carmen went home armed with this drama-releasing mantra, along with some specific talking points to help Evie see *her relationship* with others is not based on how they treat *other people*. It's based on how they *actually* treat only her. She's not responsible for how other people treat other people, only for how she acts and how she is treated.

Empowering Evie with the Magic Mantra allowed her to release taking on the behavior of others and focus on what she had control over. She had the control to act, to focus on facts and to choose who she spent her time with. The rest was not of her concern and not her responsibility. With Carmen's counsel, Evie began to understand no one else's narrative is in charge of her relationships. She began choosing to spend more time with her new friends and moved away from the drama and anxiety her old friends brought to her.

That was several years ago. Evie is a senior in high school now, and Carmen has told me she still uses the Magic Mantra all the time, and, in fact, everyone in the family uses it. "The Magic Mantra became a kind of family tradition!"

Magic Mantra Self-Reflections

1. Are you willing to let go of always being "in charge" of your kids?
2. Are you currently engaged in drama because you are attached to the outcome of someone else's situation?
3. Can you imagine ways in which the Magic Mantra will free you from problems you thought were yours?

Magic Mantra Gamechangers

Try writing this mantra down every day for a week as a way to begin applying and benefiting from it.

Set a day when you are going to consciously practice your Magic Mantra all day long. Say it aloud when you can, say it in your mind at all other times. Make sure that you invest in it. Mean it.

In every situation with your children, repeat the mantra before, during, and after… and mean it.

In every situation with your colleagues, life partner, family, friends, and acquaintances - practice the Mantra as consciously and consistently as you possibly can.

If you feel frustration, say the Mantra and then notice the possible solutions to your frustration that come to mind.

If you are waiting on someone or feeling dependent on their decision, say the Mantra and notice the choices that come to mind.

At the end of the day, take time to reflect on the effects the Magic Mantra had on your day. Consider the changes you can make throughout all aspects of your life using the Magic Mantra.

Takeaway Tool

I'm Only in Charge of Me;
I'm Not in Charge of You.

One of many gag photos, making fun of my college roommate for being engaged in college

First date, Purdue University, 1988

His name starts with 'T' and he wears a uniform

Wedding, Northport, NY, 1993

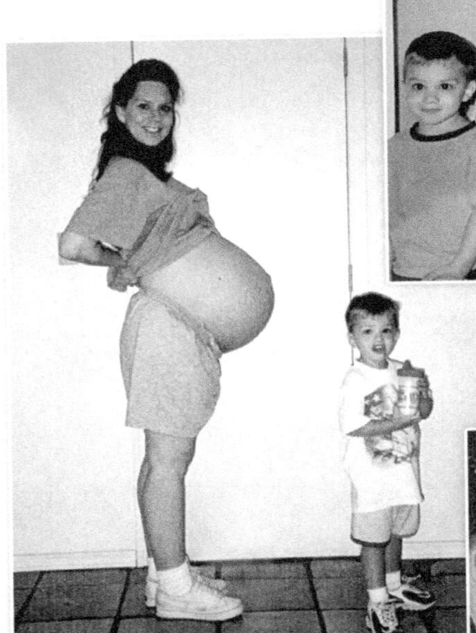

What pregnant with triplets looks like

Matt 3; Scott, Kelly and Derek 1 month;
Sue 35; Tim 34

Daddy's home from combat, it's 3 a.m., 2003

The days of "nunya business" questions, with strangers sticking their face into the carrier and asking, "Are these triplets?"

Dining Room as a makeshift playpen ... connected pet fences for large, safe play area, and sheets sewn together to protect carpet

Home from deployment, 2007

Hiking, bellies full of pancakes, tactical swear word required

Family today ... blessed

PART TWO

YOUR RELATIONSHIP WITH YOUR CHILD

Chapter 8

The Power of We; Why Being Your Child's Partner Works

"I don't want you to save me, I want you to stand by my side as I save myself."
~ Sushil Singh

A partner is defined as a pair of people engaged together in the same activity. That is the perfect way to describe the relationship between a parent and child. With a partnership mentality, we get to engage with our children, talking *with* them, rather than *at* them. The simple difference is when we talk *at* our child, we make demand statements. When we talk *with* our child, we make collaborative statements.

The Word "We" Gets A Lot Done

If you are being asked to make something, wouldn't you rather hear "when can we get this made" versus "you need to make this?" Even if you aren't personally involved in making anything, using the word "we" softens the blow of requesting something of your child, preventing a demand statement from being made. When you want your child to do something for you more willingly, use the word "we," not "you."

PS: *This worked with my husband, too, until he figured me out. "When are we going to get the vacuuming done?" It was a good run while it lasted.*

The word "you" is a lonely word, it's a one-way word. Using "we" means I am in step with my child, in tune with what he is doing, feeling, and thinking. It subliminally communicates that we are in this together. We are partners in the process. Partners interact with consideration and courtesy toward one another. Partners communicate freely and they actively listen to one another. Partners don't punish each other when they disagree or misunderstand. They search for common ground and explain themselves more clearly with reasoning if needed.

The traditional idea of parenting tends to pit parent against child. The parent is supposed to have all the answers. It's the parent's "job" to change the child's behavior. Many of us grew up thinking that parenting amounted to: I'm the parent, therefore, I'm the boss and I'm right, you're just a kid who knows nothing. That stifling, antiquated parenting model can easily leave kids feeling minimized, undervalued, and powerless.

We can't change anyone's behavior, we can only modify our own. Kids react to us. Remember: change yourself, and *then* your child changes. I'm teaching the parent to change their behavior, not fix their child's. There is a subtle distinction in that sentence. As leaders to our kids, we change the course and the child follows suit. When left without leadership from the parent, kids become confused. They don't know any better, they are adults in training.

I can facilitate and support my child as he changes, but I don't have to have all the answers. Which is a good thing, because I don't! No one does. My child doesn't need to think I have all the answers in order for me to be a good parent. When I treat my child as a partner, he knows he has the power to create his own answers. He organically learns to search for mutually beneficial solutions to any problem and he becomes a courteous, fair-minded collaborator.

Through collaboration, we gain valuable insights into our child because he feels listened to and supported, so he shares more with us. Those insights give us a jump on being able to see predictive indicators in our child's behavior. That alliance with our child is invaluable to our role as a parent. If our child feels like we are partnering with her, it results in a relationship of trust, at every age. With trust comes honesty. That connection gives us the intel we need to keep our child in her lane while she's learning.

Mutual Cooperation

Parenting as a partner allows us to meet our child at whatever level he's at, at that moment. A child is more apt to listen to us, show us respect and learn from us when we make an effort to enter his world as a teammate on the same team. If you want his cooperation, you need to give him cooperation. It's essential to remember that a child is a person, a person who will respond in kind to the way they are treated, no matter what their age.

When we parent as a partner, we discuss problems mutually, not preachily. No kid wants to hear a sermon from his parent. If you want him to listen, keep it brief and relevant to the issue.

Then follow up with non-threatening questions. "How did you feel about that?" "Have I explained this clearly?"

Partnerships influence and guide, they don't force. You might think you are doing what's best for your child when you respond in controlling ways (restricting wardrobe choices, limiting time with friends, or barring participation in certain activities) but she will view your corrections as a nonverbal invitation to rebel, argue, and misbehave. Rebellion in most forms is easy to avoid if you are partnership parenting.

The doors of communication will be kept open during the teen years if a partnership relationship has been developed while the child is young. If the child is a teen when the partnership starts, it may well take a little time for them to really trust the process. The key with teens, and with all ages actually, is consistency. As long as once you start the process it becomes something they can depend on, they will adapt quickly and tensions and frustrations will drop exponentially.

Taking the Leap

In each situation you encounter, just take the leap, and don't be afraid to have a "trust your gut" moment. When you try being less parental and more partner, it will work no matter what the circumstance.

I understand taking on a partnership role might initially seem either intimidating, as if you might lose command, or overcatering, as if you are giving in, but neither are true. It's clear by now I'm not a proponent of kissing our kids' asses. On occasion, I told mine to "suck it up" or "lose my number" when the demands became too much. By using the power of we, demanding situations are greatly reduced and our role as a parent is not diminished. In fact, it gets reinforced as a collaborator.

Skip the Convenience and Get the Lasting Connection

Granted, negotiating, and collaborating takes time and effort. As busy, stressed parents, it often seems like it's easier to just say no so the immediate problem goes away, rather than take time to brainstorm how it can work for all. But what seems convenient and easy right now, can lead to a long-lasting disconnect between us and our child. This parenting gig lasts a long time, and if we go through the whole 18+ year process jumping to the quick easy no, we'll be stuck in a vicious cycle where rebellion is the only way our kids feel like they have any power or control.

Of course, there will be situations when you make decisions without collaboration. There will be times when no means no, no questions asked. But if you have partnered with your child, they will recognize the difference in those situations and be much more able to accept the disappointing or frustrating situations when they arise because they trust you are completely invested in their well-being. They know your decisions are made for a reason rather than arbitrarily. By challenging ourselves to be a partner with our child, we will be astounded at how quickly our relationship will feel connected and in step with each other.

CASE STUDY – The Power of We. Partnership Parenting.

Mom: Carrie. 2 Daughters, 14, 11; 1 Son, 12

Carrie is a very recent client whose children were driving her crazy. Her son, Mike (12) and her daughters Bailey (14) and Maggie (11) constantly demanded Carrie be their chauffeur for social activities. Their continual demands for rides to and from anything they were doing after school or on weekends were a huge burden on her time. These requests were often unplanned and made when Carrie was in the middle of things. Carrie easily managed chauffeuring Bailey around when she was the only child old enough for a social life, but once Mike and Maggie became social, it quickly became overwhelming. Carrie lectured and even yelled about respecting her time, all to no avail.

She recently turned to ultimatums and restrictions, like, "If you put me in this position again, not only am I not driving you, but you're grounded!" This pseudo-boundary took only hours for the kids to cross… and even less time for her to cave on. Conversations with her kids were breaking down and she felt like the enemy.

The solution was actually a very simple one. I helped Carrie craft a specifically worded partnership conversation template. From that moment forward, her response to the kids' requests sounded more like this, "I have a problem that I need your help with. I don't have time to make dinner for the family and also take you back and forth to your friend's house. How can we solve that?"

By soliciting their thoughts and being their partner, Carrie invited the kids to find a workable solution. As a result, the kids asked their friend's parent to drive one way, rather than burdening Carrie with driving both ways, or they decided to ride their bike, or maybe even skip the plans altogether. By sharing her time constraints with the kids, Carrie taught them to understand her value and respect her time while she manages everyone's needs. Using the partnership strategy helped Carrie teach her kids valuable problem-solving skills, respect Carrie's time more and best of all, it got results without yelling, grounding, or lecturing.

Partnering Self-Reflections

1. Are you making demand statements? ("Get this picked up," "Finish this now," "You're going.").
2. What is the pattern you learned growing up? Do you believe you need to have all the answers to be a good parent?
3. What are some personal potential benefits you can see to becoming a partnership parent?
4. Can you think of situations where you didn't use partnership parenting, but could have for a better outcome?

Partnering Gamechangers

1. List some demanding statements you regularly use.
2. Rewrite them into a "we" statement.
3. Are there frustrating situations you currently experience that take your time and effort for granted, such as driving all the time or not getting help with chores?

Pick one to bring up to your child as a problem you would like their help with.

Takeaway Tool

We are on the same team!

Chapter 9

Respect. Are You Really Showing It?

"Respect is one of the greatest expressions of love." ~ Miguel Angel Ruiz

The Power of We and Respect are naturally interrelated. Using The Power of We will automatically have us on our way to showing our kids Respect. One builds upon the other.

Our best intentions are always to be good parents. Over the years, when working with parents, I usually begin by asking them if they felt they showed respect to their child. As expected, 100% of them said, "Yes," immediately, without hesitation, while looking at me like; "What a dumb question."

However, if you take a poll and ask any child, especially a teenager, "What do you want most from your parents?" Hands down, kids will tell you they want respect from their parents. This implies they don't feel like they are getting it.

Showing respect nurtures, and directly results in, building self-confidence. Self-confidence is one of the most critically important qualities we can cultivate in our children. Sadly, from what I've seen, self-confidence is predominantly missing in many of the kids I have met. Especially girls. The decisions some kids make, simply because they don't believe or trust in themselves, needlessly puts them in harm's way or adds unnecessary pain, suffering, and anxiety to their lives. It takes years for them to acquire confidence in themselves on their own.

As parents, we have the chance to save them that time and anguish by treating our kids with respect. Doing so gives our children a jumpstart in life. Respect is the main ingredient to partnership parenting and to having kids who are independent, emotionally balanced, and self-confident.

What Respect Isn't

Let's first talk about what respect isn't:

1. It's not getting on the floor and playing whenever your child asks because he's bored. Bored is a fixable state of mind. A great favor we can do for our kids is to consistently challenge them to keep their brain creating, learning, and discovering. By making it clear that it's our child's responsibility to fix boredom, not ours, they become resilient, creative, self-sufficient individuals.
2. It's not thinking you need to be "Disneyland Parent," entertaining your child, having events scheduled back to back over the weekends so he's always happily busy. Children need to know how to entertain themselves and create happiness in their own lives, not depend on others for their happiness.
3. It's not listening endlessly, bent down looking him in the eye with your undivided attention *every single time* he talks. Those are nice touches when you are able, but they

aren't necessary to being a good parent who shows respect. Let's be honest, every thought they have is not of equal importance. But if your world stops every time they speak, they grow to expect that. They develop a sense of entitlement. What they are really learning is a lack of respect for your time and attention. Children learn that "not right now" means they can wait until we are ready to give them our attention. My kids knew I worked, ran a home, and took time to care for myself. Kids need to be aware they are a part of the whole.

4. It's not being an over-pleasing parent. It might feel good to do it, but being over-pleasing sets your child up for disappointment when interacting with others; like teachers, coaches, and eventually bosses. If your child feels like she is always your star child and can do no wrong, she will be robbed of the necessary coping skills in the real world. This is similar to the "participation medal" scenarios where kids in recent generations have all been trained to believe they should get a trophy just for showing up. Over-pleasing at home creates a child opposite of whom we hope to create; it creates a child who does not feel self-worthy, one who feels she has to comply with others to please them and one who cannot be given constructive feedback to better herself.

It's a good thing that we've already learned to get our ego out of the way and let go of control, because this is the place where the rubber meets the road. If our parenting is based in fear or control, we cannot possibly be showing respect. And, when our ego is front and center, fear and control are running the show. Expressing respect is impossible when we are scared or busy clamping down on non-essential rules. When we up-level our game of removing our ego and letting go of control, showing respect becomes our default response.

Respect is at the root of all interaction with another person. It's a basic courtesy we use daily but oftentimes it goes out the window with those closest to us or those we have control over, like our kids. Have you noticed how we tend to treat complete strangers better than we do our kids, spouse, or sibling? We find nicer ways to say no or disagree with strangers but take liberties with our family. With those close to us, we feel like, "Oh, they know what I meant."

You will not automatically be respected by your child simply by being her parent. It's earned on both sides. Just acknowledging that sentence as true is a great start. Kids are the only ones in our family who get a double whammy. We take liberties with them as with other members of our family and we also think we need to have control over them. Remember, your child is their own person and is figuring out life for themself and needs the space to do that.

Showing Respect Boils Down to Two Basic Concepts

With the majority of my parenting in the rearview mirror, I have the advantage of hindsight being 20/20. While parenting four kids, who are worthy adversaries with their confidence and strong opinions, I had the essence of respect down to two basic concepts: ***Know When You're Winning and Say Nothing*** and ***Respectful Engagement.*** If you use these concepts, they will work within the hour, regardless of your child's age.

CONCEPT #1: Know When You're Winning and Say Nothing

Generations of parents have passed down the advice to pick our battles. But oftentimes, when we are in the moment, we need more than that.

Thinking in terms of picking a battle implies there is a winner and a loser. The truth is, if you use the Say Nothing; Know When You're Winning concept, everybody wins. When people refer to the parenting technique of picking your battles, they're usually suggesting that you pick which bad behavior to completely overlook and which to allow. But if you address questionable behavior strategically and focus on your wins in the moment, then you'll never lose, you'll just consciously prioritize your wins.

Using some common scenarios, here are a few examples of how the Know When You're Winning and Say Nothing concept works in action.

Leave Them Alone, With Conscious Intention

It wasn't until I started leaving my kids alone that they truly started to flourish. Ironically, respecting your child by leaving him alone, is actually one of the *Secrets to Parenting Without Giving a F^ck.*

As parents, we can have certain expectations. The trick is to realize that after stating our intent, we need to leave them alone. Our good intentions can unwittingly sabotage our efforts when we continually preach lessons, make demands, or nag.

Scenario #1: Say you ask your toddler to put her toys away. She throws a fit but starts slowly putting toys in the bucket, while still throwing a little fit. You are winning. Say nothing. Of course you feel like you need to "correct" the fit-like behavior. But don't. Because you are winning, *she's doing what you asked.* Tell yourself to leave her alone, as long as she continues to put her toys away.

Scenario #2: Before breakfast, you ask your ten-year old son to empty the dishwasher. He's grumbling under his breath—while actually walking over to the dishwasher to do it—"this is crap, they make me do everything!!" You want to tell him to piss off and stop talking back. Should you? No. You are winning. Say nothing. *He's emptying the dishwasher, like you asked.*

Scenario #3: Your daughter is mowing the lawn. She is supposed to bag the grass but doesn't. You tell her to go back out there and go over the lawn again, this time with the grass catcher attached. She is furious she has to do it over! She stomps back out there accusing you of being the worst parent ever. She has friends waiting to meet up with her. But she is walking back out there to do the j-o-b. Do you address the backtalk? No, you do not. You are winning. Say nothing.

It's so tempting to feel like we need to be the parent who corrects *all* questionable behavior. In those moments we overdo our parenting. The reverse happens: kids fixate on the negative corrections. They just want acknowledgment from us of whatever good they are doing. Our kids don't realize the impact of their backtalk on us. The effort it took for them to do what we ask gets undermined by us overparenting that moment—that is all the child will remember, that feeling of being unappreciated.

That's why the concept of Know When You're Winning, Say Nothing is effective. I've said it before, but it's worth repeating - never pass up the opportunity to shut the f^ck up.

This idea works in the big picture, too, not just in the moment. Let's say your child's bathroom is a mess, always dirty with towels on the floor and a sink full of toothpaste and you can't get him to keep it clean. Ask yourself, is everything else going well? Is he doing a sport or playing an instrument? Is he doing well in school? Is he coming home on time? Does he have a great group of friends? You are winning, let the bathroom go.

Sometimes we have to remind ourselves of all the good and not fixate on the one bad thing. Many, many times my husband and I needed to check those boxes with each other to nudge ourselves toward keeping the big picture if we were harping on one bad, inconsequential behavior.

Learning to recognize when we are winning helps us overlook which behavior is not as relevant and which behavior we need to focus on so we don't find fault with everything.

By showing my child respect, we both feel good. If I choose to overlook certain behavior (mumbled backtalk, mini-fit being thrown,) I must also achieve cooperation on certain other behavior (toys picked up, dishwasher emptied, lawn mowed and bagged.) If I'm getting results, I'm willing to ignore the lesser behavior (messy bathroom.)

Their Grades are Their Business

Grades are a big source of contention in many families. My personal take on grades is to make them a non-issue. My grades were horrible until I got to college and found something to study that interested me. No amount of anything my mom could have said or done would have changed my performance in high school. I was always grateful to her for staying out of it. She was right to do so. I ended up on the dean's list at a small university in Connecticut, then transferred and graduated from Purdue University. I did it proudly all on my own, without being browbeaten by my parents under the guise of "parenting" me.

Things work out the way they are meant to. You don't need to ride your kid, starting at age ten, for excellent grades. Yes, I know the stakes are high if you have bad grades and a low GPA in high school. But whose life is it? Any unrelenting intervention and constant reminders cause needless stress and anxiety in a child. They figure it out themselves, they really do.

All the hand-holding and effort it takes to push a child toward having great grades is exhausting for both the child and the parent. It creates a child who feels defeated and inadequate, not a child who feels self-empowered. It's disrespectful. By pushing him, he gets the message from his parent, "You can't do this without me," and, "I don't believe for a second you can do this." That is ego parenting at work, as well as control.

Since our oldest is like me in many ways, I knew how to read him. My husband began bugging him freshman year of high school to "get upstairs and study," asking, "Did you finish that paper?" and "What was your grade on the algebra test?" Then it turned into telling him *how* to study and *when* to study. My husband was fully convinced he was doing the right thing as a parent. But I recognized our son's reaction (it would have been mine exactly) and gently told my husband to stop. Leave him alone and watch what happens.

That night he left him alone and every night thereafter. As expected, the freedom from being badgered worked miracles. Matt started caring on his own. He became engaged in talking to teachers, figuring out assignments and asking pertinent questions. None of that curiosity is present when a child is being told what to ask rather than being allowed to discover it for themselves. All his energy would have continued going into dodging Dad. Instead, he began to feel respected. To this day, my husband credits that advice with saving his relationship with our son. He would have kept upping the ante, inviting a power struggle in the name of parenting, and who really had the power? Our son. He had the power to not study, to get bad grades and to make Dad angry. If a child feels challenged in an environment in which he feels no support, all his energy will go into defending himself, rather than into learning. What a waste of effort. A little respect goes a long way. The power of leaving kids alone is real.

CONCEPT #2: Respectful Engagement

While establishing the foundation of respect with our child, there will be times where we say nothing and there will be times where we need to engage. When we do, we want that engagement to be respectful.

Here are a few examples of how the Respectful Engagement concept works in action:

"I Told You So's"

Our son Derek came home from school saying he needed a notebook for a specific class. The notebook needed to perform certain functions. I recommended a specific style notebook, based on my business presentations and explained all the reasons why it would meet his needs. He was a brand-new driver, eager to go purchase it himself. At the store, he made another choice based on what he thought was best. When he showed it to me, I said nothing. His teacher did not accept the one he purchased and told him to get the one I recommended.

I wanted to shout from the rooftops "I soooo told you! I guess Mom knows a few things." But I stopped myself. Refrain from calling out the obvious with jabs or critiques. No one, including us, wants to be reminded of a mistake or bad choice we made. As parents, we need to resist closing the loop and making that jab. When your ego is truly not involved, you will have the restraint to not to say, "I told you so."

Nit-Picking

I saw a mom and her son at the store. He stood nearby with his hands in his pocket, doing nothing. His harried mom, while not even looking at him, kept saying, "So and so, get over here, don't touch anything…I said *get over here now.*" That mom just needed to come up for air and focus a seconds-worth of respectful attention on her son to see his behavior was perfectly fine. He didn't need to be nit-picked.

Nit-picking is the fastest way for you to have your child not listen to you. We never want to give our kids more reasons to tune us out.

Value His Time

Everything is relative. We think we are busy and kids think they are busy. All we know is what we know. It's not up to us to decide what constitutes busy-ness. If he's having down time that he carved space for, then he is busy. We don't want to minimize his decisions about how he spends his time, as we don't want him to minimize our decisions about how we spend ours. Acknowledge that his time is important to him and to you. If you need his assistance with something, ask, "Are you available to help me tonight?" or, "What is your schedule tomorrow, I need some help putting together that table. Will you be around?"

Showing respect for his time ensures he will show respect for yours. These tiny gestures to engage with respect are incredibly appreciated and noticed by your child. They pay huge dividends in your relationship.

Being Strict Lacks Creativity

Taking pride in being a strict parent does not equal being a good parent. It's easy to be strict, all it takes is saying no all the time, using words like *can't*, and *don't*. Being strict just to be strict is simply fear masquerading as control and restriction. It's not partnership parenting and it's not respectful. Frankly, being strict lacks creativity. None of the parents we knew who were overly strict had fun, happily functioning relationships with their child. If you are super-strict, your child doesn't feel that she can be honest with you for fear of disappointing you or being punished. Mutual respect has not been established. Being strict is one-way street parenting. It's practically an invitation asking your child to rebel.

Expectations

Having an exhaustive list of expectations could unknowingly be putting your child at risk for anxiety. Having many expectations does not translate to showing respect. It simply means you are teaching her she only has significance if she pleases you and does what you deem as important. Respect requires empathy to strike the balance between expecting too little and expecting too much. That's the *conscious intention* part of leaving them alone.

Conversely, having no expectations also shows no respect. If your toddler falls and bumps her head and cries, respect her enough to say, "Try again, you can do it!"

Privacy is Paramount

If you choose to go through your child's phone and social media, that should be a condition discussed prior to allowing your child to set up the account. She should know with complete transparency that you will check her accounts by asking her to hand over the appliance. You won't be looking at her accounts without her present. Snooping behind her back is never respectful or good parenting. It's also not what a respectful partner would do. The violation a child feels by a parent going through her personal items, without her knowledge, absolutely never goes away.

The Power of We & Respect Combine to Solve Most Problems

When the Power of We is incorporated with Showing Respect we possess a nearly unbeatable set of parenting problem-solving skills. These two skill sets combined will make a huge difference in how you parent and how quickly and consistently you get results.

If we notice our ego is engaged, we are guilting our child, or we are imposing control, we now recognize those character traits as signals to use "we" language to bring the relationship back to respect.

These first two chapters in Part Two turn a very important corner in how you will interact with your child. By incorporating "we" into conversations, one-way interactions turn into two-way respectful interactions.

CASE STUDY – Respect.

Dad: Pete. 1 Daughter, 13

My client Pete was experiencing the age-old "clean your room" dilemma with his daughter Kelcey (13). It took hours for Kelcey to do a miniscule amount of cleaning. Frustrated, Pete found himself hovering over her with 'helpful' phrases like, "What's taking so long?" "You should be done by now!" and "Don't you know how to pick up your stuff?" Pete didn't realize his mounting frustration became power fuel for his daughter. An important tip I share with many parents is this: *It's easy for your child to get power and control by not doing something that you want them to do.*

Pete needed to immediately remove himself from the power struggle. I had him withdraw from the process of *how* it gets done and just expect it to *be* done. I had to assure Pete that, though it may not feel like it, when you remove yourself from how, and just expect them to figure it out, respect is shown. Once the boundaries and expectations are established and clearly communicated, Dad exits. Without Dad's hovering, reminding, and commenting, Kelcey became free to see that her room cleaning took up her entire day. She realized how much time she wasted in her room, trying *not* to clean. At that point, she did what she needed to do and got on with it.

Pete focused on respecting his daughter's process and he found cleaning her room did not become a 'thing' after that. He let go of control, respectfully not giving a f^ck, with conscious intention. The room still got cleaned, even if it took her an hour or all day. Pete's expectation was for her to clean her room today. This technique allowed Pete to feel like he's not a bad parent with a bad daughter. It's a simple matter of showing respect.

Respect Self-Reflections

1. Do you speak to and negotiate with your child as you would with another adult?
2. Do you value your child's time as their own, rather than a subset of yours?
3. Do you feel that your child's successes or failures reflect on you as a parent?
4. Do you know what your child thinks is their greatest challenge?

Respect Gamechangers

1. Pick one area where you tend to nag or control rather than respect, like cleaning the room. Write it at the top of a page and make three columns below it.
   a. Column 1: List your child's typical responses and reactions to being asked or commanded to do that task.
   b. Column 2: For each of their responses and reactions in column 1 - list your corresponding typical nagging or controlling reaction.
   c. Column 3 - For each of your controlling reactions list a respectful alternative that leaves them alone.
2. Pick a demand or requirement you have of your child that tends to lead to frustration in your relationship.
   a. Sit down with your child and discuss what it is that frustrates them.
   b. Try to listen without ego. In other words, during the discussion, keep it about them, rather than you.

Takeaway Tool

"Leave them alone, with conscious intention."

Chapter 10

How to Get Your Kids to Tell You Everything

"I have found the best way to give advice to your children is to find out what they want and then advise them to do it." ~ Harry S. Truman

So many parents have told me they wished they had a better relationship with their child. The kind of relationship where their child tells them everything. Being so bogged down in the daily parental grind, they woke up one day and felt like they were missing a connection with their child. Being connected is a different feeling than just being their parent. Even though we see our child every day, we still might be left out of knowing their thoughts, hopes and feelings.

We are the ones responsible for establishing rules and reinforcing lessons. Unfortunately, we often find ourselves having unconsciously traded those rules for true intimate communication with our children. But this is not an either/or situation. We can do both. We need to do both. It is possible to be the parent who balances boundary-setting with fostering trust and dialogue with our child. Trusted dialogue is sparked and then stoked. It's through a specific style of interaction with our child that meaningful communication and a deep relationship evolves.

Follow these four strategies to get your kid singing like a canary:

Strategy #1: Brand Yourself as Unshockable

Start by branding yourself as the person who is willing to talk about anything. From as young as your child can remember, they should think of you as someone who will talk about anything, listen to anything and laugh at anything. Nothing shocks you.

If your child is young, great, you can start early and set it up from the beginning. But if your child is older, then start now. See Strategy #2.

Getting there will require suffering through awkward angst and embarrassment from your child. He will try to throw you off your brand. He will act disinterested, disgusted, and maybe even in disbelief.

But soldier on. Once you break through the clutter, and his walls come down, your value as a trusted and open-minded resource gets cemented.

The goal is to become skilled at strategic, casual conversation with your child so she *wants* to share her daily experiences with you. A great way to start the process is by first showing her you are unflappable.

Strategy #2: Use Indirect References

Any time we want to reach our child to get a lesson through or change a behavior, they will be more apt to listen if we use indirect references. Talking to them using third-party examples makes our lessons seem less directed at them personally. When they don't feel like they are on the hot seat, they are less defensive and more willing to listen to us. Here are three ways indirect references can be used as conversation starters:

Share Your Own Personal Stories and Mistakes: Be willing to discuss sensitive or embarrassing stories about yourself. It makes kids feel safe telling us their fears, concerns and humiliating moments. I call this process "pimping myself." I'd happily throw myself under the bus any day to get an important point across to my kids. I don't care. Not for a second.

I was amazed to see the fun reaction my kids had to me sharing stories from my past mistakes or bad decisions on any topic we were discussing. They loved hearing my escapades and asking me questions. Telling our personal stories humanizes us and bridges the gap between us and our child by sharing parts of ourselves as a person, not just as a parent.

I know this is a tough one for some parents. It feels like you might look foolish or lose status with your kids. Many parents have told me they flat out rejected telling their kids anything about their past, and I know you might feel that way too. But trust me, a little bit of embarrassment is well worth the invaluable opportunity for the deep bonding (and laughing) you'll experience with your child by using yourself as the example of what not to do!

When we candidly lay ourselves bare, our child feels comfortable with his own disclosures, and, after all, isn't that what we are after? By sharing our own private tales, we eliminate the judgement our child thinks we will have against him for a similar adventure.

Share Examples from Other Known People: Where your own personal stories might be lacking, use examples from other people. Our kids had proven they were trustworthy with keeping information private. I felt comfortable, when applicable, sharing little gossipy stories of other people if I thought it would benefit the situation they were going through. They love being let in on a secret about other adults, whether it be an old friend or a neighbor. (Yes kids, you saw our neighbor being driven home in a cab. She got arrested for drinking and driving.) The story and lesson write itself.

Showing you trust them to keep information private provides a bonding moment between you that will allow your point to get made, indirectly. Talking about someone else sometimes gets them to share more with us than they anticipated. Maybe after hearing the above example, my daughter might now feel comfortable telling me her friend's dad also drinks too much and when she slept over it scared her to see him behave that way. Now I have new information I didn't have before. No more sleep overs at Becca's house!

Share Articles and News Stories: Ripping out articles or sharing news stories provides another neutral source of information where the focus isn't on them. Indirectly referring to a stranger's experience allows for comfortable and safe communication because it's not about them. I was more apt to get them talking if it was about an arbitrary person.

I never wasted the chance to show our kids how others got hurt not wearing their helmet or how texting and driving can be deadly. It worked wonders to be able to show them that what happened to other kids could also happen to them. Reading an article isn't mom harping and lecturing, it's an actual event they can learn from. The indirect reference is gold in getting kids to listen and talk.

After all these years, I've had the privilege of seeing how my efforts cutting out articles and sharing stories eventually made the lessons sink in. I've overheard the kids quoting the news story to their friends or offering the lesson as advice to a friend as if it were their own observation. Sometimes, even months later, one of the kids referred back to a story I assumed they'd forgotten about. Those efforts also paid off in keeping conversations flowing. Even when teenage eyes rolled at the regular flow of articles, they now freely admit to being grateful for the open communication it reinforced.

Strategy #3: Use Logic, Not Emotion

It's human nature. If your child thinks you are too emotionally invested in something you want him to do or say, he will do the opposite or do nothing at all. For some reason, kids seem to reject emotional pleas from their parents. If we are too interested, it turns them off. Thus, there is all the more reason to use the appearance of not giving a f^ck as an effective tool. Too much fear, negativity, or positivity for any idea is met with disgust and inaction or the wrong reaction. The way around that is using logic, taking the emotion out of conversations.

To think logically, put your ego in hiding, your controlling ways under control, and make feelings of guilt a thing of the past. Using logic makes conversations simple, reasonable, and not overly personal. Feelings are not facts; kids don't want to listen to our emotional psycho-babble. Once you've broached a subject, whether you used yourself as an example or whether you just need to talk about a sensitive subject, here are the next steps in getting your child to talk:

Be non-judgmental: One of the greatest compliments my daughter ever gave me was telling me I never made her feel judged, no matter what she told me. It surprised me to hear that because I tend to be a bit over-the-top Italian with my reactions. What her words told me was that we judge ourselves harder than our kids judge us. The easiest way to be non-judgmental is to not lecture. Avoid hammering her with lessons if she is sharing.

We feel so compelled to lecture. We all do it and we don't recognize it. If we show judgement, it makes a child feel as if she has to defend her position. In the defensive position, she digs her heels in deeper, justifying her faulty logic. If she's digging in, she is completely shut off to my message. We feel we have limited time to get any lessons across, so we launch into all the reasons why or why not and the child hears it as a lecture.

"Mom, I drank half of my friend's energy drink. I have a headache and I can't stop my hand from shaking." My mind is like dominoes in freefall. What I really want to do is to contort my face like WTF and snarkily say: "Why would you drink out of someone else's cup? Don't you know energy drinks are filled with so much crap that is bad for you? Of course your hand is shaking and your head hurts, it's got enough caffeine to power ten men!!!" But instead, I gather myself and calmly look at my child and say, with logic, "Yes, that stuff has stimulant ingredients meant to make you feel that way. Let's get you some water. Does your friend drink those a lot? Maybe be careful drinking out of somebody else's cup. You might end up with something worse than the jitters." Logic, no judgement, and a little information. Once I find out if her friend gulps a lot of energy drinks, I will circle back in a couple of days with a story or article about energy drinks.

Now, maybe you're thinking your child would find the follow-up article from you on energy drinks to be post-judgy. The follow-up article isn't meant to throw the drinking of energy drinks back in her face at a later date. It's meant to inform her from a non-biased third party. The secret to keeping yourself in the sharing safe-zone is in the *delivery* of the follow-up article. You are very casual, "Oh hey, saw this article about what we talked about the other day, thought you might find it interesting in case you choose to have more energy drinks." I'm not making demands, I'm not judging, I'm simply informing ...no strings attached. Casual delivery is essential to success. And as I mentioned above, they may roll their eyes and sigh over the follow-up articles, but at least I know they've seen it.

The rest is, of course, up to them. This is the real essence to the mindset of not giving a f^ck. There is acting involved, cavalier, cool, not overly invested, letting them learn the lesson. She is going to keep drinking energy drinks. But, your educational information will help her learn the lesson more quickly.

Avoid showing a surprise reaction: If your child is confiding in you, keep your emotions in check. A surprise reaction will put distance between the two of you. She will immediately shut down or feel embarrassed and stop talking if you are reacting. Acting surprised makes her feel like you cannot handle the information she is sharing.

Kids are faced with so much stressful information; they need to have a safe person to tell their stories to. If your child's friend has experienced abuse or is doing drugs, she needs to know with certainty she can trust you not to overreact.

This technique is not just for older kids. Younger children have some of the most embarrassing questions, such as asking about where babies come from or asking about sex. These are the early questions that allow us to begin branding ourselves as being willing to talk about anything. Young kids are not as easily embarrassed as pre-teens are, so take those opportunities when you get them to show you can handle it.

Be direct and open: Embrace wherever the conversation flows. Don't say, "I don't want to hear this right now," or "This is too much information." It sounds prudish and makes them think you can't deal with the truth.

Being open and truthful lays the foundation for your child to want to tell you everything. Kids are simple beings. It's adults who tend to complicate issues with our years of experiences and over-thinking. Deal directly with your child, don't be tempted to pass off the subject to your partner, teacher, friend or anyone else.

Listen like you have no place else to be: This is for when children are a bit older and are formulating concepts that need a safe place to land. Kids need the validation of knowing they have been heard. Listening as though you have no other place to be, or no other thing to be doing, gives your kids a feeling of trust and ease. Be actively engaged, not distracted on your phone or multi-tasking with some other chore. Just listening, without comment. Give her a chance to get all her feelings out. Listen as if there is no limit to how long she can talk. If she can count on you to be a good listener, she will keep telling you everything.

P.S. *Important note: This doesn't mean we have to treat everything our child says as if it has the highest level of importance. Some things they may really want to tell us are either chatter or gossip and don't require our immediate undivided attention. However, if we are regularly practicing careful listening, we will recognize the difference and our child will recognize the difference, too.*

Don't try to solve their problem: One of the most important components to listening is hearing your child without feeling the need to solve the situation. We all know how it feels to have our friends or spouse cut us off and try to solve our problem when all we wanted was for them to listen to us. Let's not do that to our child, either. Kids can't grow or learn if we feed the answers to them. We can be an ear without having to weigh in with our opinions and solutions.

We already know, if we keep solving his problems, his ability to solve his own problems becomes stifled. But beyond that, remember, this is about getting them to tell you everything... and it's a simple fact that if you are talking, your child won't be. You'll have blown the opportunity to provide what they really needed; caring and empathy. And it will be that much harder next time you attempt to get them to talk.

Don't give frivolous reassurances: Kids can smell a rat. If we give generic, robotic responses like, "It will be OK," or, "It's fine," it feels patronizing, as if what he's saying or feeling didn't deserve a customized response. To keep him talking, make a specific, thoughtful comments. No one likes to feel placated.

If your child has a disagreement with her best friend, you can ask, "Oh wow, how did you respond? What do you think you'll do now? Is there any way I can help?" Our goal is to make personalized, thoughtful responses to the information she is sharing with you.

Frivolous reassurances make frivolous conversations. They don't invite further dialogue. Giving a generic response feels unempathetic to our child and won't contribute value to the conversation.

Strategy # 4: Master the Art of Questioning

Mastering the Art of Questioning is the secret of all secrets to getting your kids to talk to you and to having a fun, trusting relationship with them. If you are only going to focus on one of these four strategies, this is the money-maker.

As a general rule, we don't ask people enough questions. Most of us love being asked questions. We love being asked about ourselves, our opinions, our feelings, how we solved a problem and most of all, we love being asked for advice. These are great points to keep in mind while chatting with our child.

Interesting fact: On average, within less than 30 seconds, people turn any conversation back to being about themselves. Most people spend 60-80% of conversations talking about themselves.[1]

Conversing with our kids involves learning a different set of probing skills to keep them talking. The best way to use these

---

[1] The Neuroscience of Everybody's Favorite Topic - Scientific American: Ward, Adrian F. July 16, 2013.

probing skills is to learn new ways of asking questions. Get ready to become a master interviewer. This is how you'll get your kids to seek you out at the end of the day so they can tell you everything.

Be genuinely curious, with a few twists: A curious parent genuinely wants to know the details, the process, the discovery of it all. Be curious though, not nosy. The best way to tell if you are being curious or being nosy is if you are curious, your child answers easily, if you are being nosy, your child balks at answering or gets visibly uncomfortable.

Being nosy feels more like an invasion to him: "Who is that you are texting?" "What is he saying?" Those types of intrusive questions set off most kids. It would me, too. It's not respectful partnership behavior on our part. If we wouldn't like to be asked the question from our significant other, it's a safe bet our kids won't like it asked of them either.

This is my favorite sentence to say when the kids get home, "Tell me everything, leave nothing out!" They know I mean it in the most genuinely curious way possible. Whenever a story started about their evening with friends, I lapped up every word like a thirsty puppy. If the story started too far in, I'd interrupt and say, "Wait, so when did you show up?" He would then have to backtrack and give me more details. I'd say, "You know I live for details." (Pimping myself takes the spotlight off the child and keeps him talking.) I'd show interest in the unfolding of his entire evening, curious about his interpretations and opinions, then I'd throw him off the interrogative scent by asking for a silly detail. "Wait, who was there? Didn't you know her from the old gymnastics days? Do you have a picture of what she looks like now?" That led to other engaging information being divulged.

The recipe for getting kids to dish more particulars than you ever thought possible, and even more than they realize: Sincere curiosity, combined with rapt attention while they speak, asking seemingly mundane details, throwing in a few silly questions, along with a little pimping of yourself on the side; and voila! Secret spilling commences. All you have to do is file the highlights away for future reference.

Ask Agenda-less Questions: With agenda-less questions, we are trying to get a handle on *their opinions*. We want to understand the broader issues about how our kids think and feel. To do this we want to make sure our questions aren't loaded with hidden agendas. If our question implies there is a right answer, our child feels like the conversation is a trap or set-up and won't feel comfortable giving us their opinion. Having an implied agenda on our end does not encourage loose and comfortable conversation with our child. She needs to feel like her answer is right because it's her answer. She will keep talking if she doesn't feel lured into trying to figure out what it is we want her to say.

When we ask a question with an implied agenda, we are giving away what we are *really* thinking and what we really want to know. Any question with an agenda won't help us figure out our child's real thoughts on the matter. If they sense a motive from us, they will sidestep the question and give us some BS answer, and that will be the end of the conversation.

An example of an agenda question is, "Do you think you should be able to drink at 18 instead of 21?" That is a yes or no question with an implied agenda where the child knows the right answer you want to hear. An alternative agenda-less question would be, "What age do you think people should be able to drink?" This invites them to give their personal opinion without an implication of what you think.

Another agenda question is, "Can you believe she married at age 20?" The parent's opinion is inherent here. There is no option for the child to say anything other than no or to disagree with the parent. The alternative here is, "How old do you think someone should be when they get married?" Then let your child talk freely without any reaction or follow-up agenda-filled questions.

Once we elicit our child's honest responses, we don't want to pull a bait and switch by pouncing with our opinions and judgement after they've exposed their true feelings. The intention with these questions is twofold: to engage, build trust and help our child develop their own judgement and intuition; and to file away what you learn so you can steer future conversations toward topics you feel they need more guidance on.

Think of this chapter as getting your advanced degree in parenting!

Ask Non-Direct Questions: The quickest way to put our kids on mute is to ask a direct question. With a direct question, our child typically has to pick between the truth or a lie. He will select whichever is the least confrontational. Backing our kids into a corner with a direct question ensures an open-and-shut conversation, not a confiding conversation.

"Did you hit your brother?" "Would you lie to me like your friend does to his Mom?" "Was there alcohol there?" There are no easy answers here for a child. These on-the-spot, threatening-type questions put our child in a no-win scenario. Asking direct questions serves up lies on a silver platter.

Tip: If you want to be lied to, ask a direct question.

Try these alternatives: "What do you think happened to your brother? Why would he be crying?" This invites engagement and is open-ended enough for you to keep questioning if needed.

"Why do you think your friend lies to his Mom? It's too bad he feels he has to do that. I will always be on your side when you tell me the truth." This question solicits his observations about why he thinks his friend lies and then follows up with a reassuring statement encouraging him that he will be protected and safe telling you the truth.

"If there is alcohol there, will you promise me you will be careful?" With this question you are not directly addressing the alcohol because it's not necessary, you are assuming there will be. (Yes, there will be!) With our veiled assumption alcohol will be there, we indicate our understanding of what she is facing at parties and then ask her to promise to be careful. This will keep dialogue open, there is no need to ask a direct question about alcohol just to get her talking. Approaching sensitive subjects circuitously is how we keep her from shutting us out.

Many times, we aren't going to get the full answer with one or two questions. If we're probing suspected bad behavior, we have to ask questions in phases and accumulate the information. Here is an example of an agenda vs agenda-less question if you are fairly certain your pre-teen snuck out last night. An agenda question in this case is: "How much sleep did you get last night?" He likely knows what you are doing or suspects you know something. Instead try, "You look really tired today for some reason, are you feeling OK?" He responds, "Yes, I'm fine." To which you say, "Just checking, I heard some noises late last night and wondered if you were awake and it was you."

We might not get the truth right away, but much of parenting, especially with pre-teens and teens, is about keeping lines of communication open.

Non-direct questioning can generate information gathering for later use while waiting for the right opportunity to reapproach the subject. At least now he knows you heard him. Parenting requires a layered approach. We shouldn't expect that asking questions will solve our parenting problems that minute. Our goal with questions is to get them talking to us and trusting us.

Stay Accusation-Free: Asking questions with an accusatory tone has a tinge of inherent judgement. The overwhelming feeling our child experiences from an accusation question is a lack of trust from us. If we are asking, "Where did you go?" "Who were you with?" or "Why did you go back to that guy that dumped you?" These types of questions feel like grilling. They don't feel like we are genuinely curious about what our child is doing.

To keep the accusatory tone out, try broadening the questions: "Did you go somewhere fun?" It's not as forthright as, "Where did you go?" By adding the word fun, it distracts from the real reason we are asking, which is to find out where they went. "Who all was there?" Asking who *all* was there does not demand to know which person he was specifically with. Rewording the question and adding the word "all" removes the implication that I might not approve of the person he was with.

Expanding the question allows for more information to be shared while not feeling as if he is on the hotseat. "How did you two decide to get back together?" Adding "you two" takes the focus off your child and asking "how they decided" encourages more than a one-word answer. The goal is to get insight into their thought process without feeling like they are being judged.

Use Questions to Guide: Asking guiding questions attempts to lead our child down a path of self-discovery so she thinks it's her idea. Guiding questions are also my personal favorite for teaching empathy and lessons.

Bullies: If your child bullies another child, instead of saying, "You won't be liked if you bully other kids." Try asking guiding questions such as, "How do you think other kids feel toward a bully? If a bully wants to have friends, what other ways are there for her to make friends?" Guiding questions help her discover the part she plays in her behavior and the consequence of her behavior on other people.

Cheating in school: If our child gets caught cheating or mentions his intent to cheat, lead him down the path of discovery. "Do you understand the material or are you just feeling too lazy to study?" "Are you aware of what the stakes are to cheating?" "Will you fail the class or get kicked out of school if you get caught?" "What are your goals for the future? Will cheating get in the way of those?" This line of questioning gets him to consider other angles and the consequences to his behavior. But, notice that at no time is there judgement or a demand to not cheat.

I realize every cell in your brain might want to scream, "Don't cheat!!!" But trust me, that won't stop anything, except your open communication line with your child. Instead, your guiding questions are helping lead them to introspection and self-awareness ("Do you understand the material?" "Are you feeling lazy?"); potential consequences (Failing? Expulsion?), and big picture thinking ("What are your goals for the future?" "Will cheating help or hurt those goals?")

Guiding questions allow us to share lessons while leading our child down the path to self-realization. They get to decide how to make those decisions without us solving the issue.

Golden Rule to Being Told Everything: Do not react. Any reaction on our part stops them from talking. The only safe reactions are no reaction, approval, or humor.

CASE STUDY – Talk About Everything.

Dad: Brian. 2 Daughters: 16, 10; 1 Son, 12

Brian's wife Angelique had been a client a couple of times over the years when she faced challenges parenting their 3 kids. When Brian discovered his 12-year old son looking at graphic porn on a shared electronic device, he felt it was his turn to come and see me. Understandably disturbed, Brian confronted his son. He took away his electronic device for two weeks and grounded him. Yet, his son continued to find ways to access the internet to view porn. Brian was upset and without any ideas except for more restrictions and punishment. This was why Angelique suggested he come and see me.

Using restriction when a child is curiously exploring doesn't work. Well, truthfully, it doesn't work in most any case. Kids don't need to feel scared or bad about their curiosity, that will only lead to them getting their answers and access somewhere else. Kids need their parents to help them navigate this increasingly dicey topic, but first they have to know that it's safe to talk to their parents, no matter what the topic. I asked Brian to think of a story he could share about himself. Every Dad remembers when he found his uncle's or his older brother's Playboy stash. Every Mom remembers some version of having a giggle-fest looking up body parts with her girlfriends. Sharing personal stories helps kids feel understood. Brian and I worked on a "script" of sorts to help establish common ground and explain porn is way more than the tantalizing photos his son viewed.

He sat his son down and began talking, this time from a partner perspective. It felt less awkward thinking in those terms, and it helped Brian ease into explaining the dangers of porn in general. He started by sharing the seedy side of porn as a business, from its addictive nature, to the harmful effects of intense inputs on the brain. Brian even tied porn to sex trafficking and explained to his son how children are being stolen to support the industry. At 12 years old, kids are able to comprehend a good portion of meaning from this type of conversation. By treating his son with the respect, having an open and forthright discussion, Brian is helping his son develop a conscience and a sense of responsibility to help protect all women, including his mom and his sisters.

Once Brian understood that restricting his electronic use and grounding him would do nothing to instill a deeper understanding or inspire compassion in the future, he realized it was his responsibility to instruct his child, help him see the big picture, and instill consistent boundaries that help his son get through this phase unscathed. As a part of their initial logical, informative conversation Brian let his son know he understood his son's curiosity, but for all the reasons discussed the behavior was unacceptable. He let his son know he is always willing talk about anything without judgement and for his safety, he would be installing blocking, filtering software on their router and check his device periodically. Interestingly, Brian reported that he got zero push back from his son and he felt like the whole ordeal ended up making them closer.

Get Your Kids to Tell You Everything Self-Reflections

1. Are there areas of life that you and your child currently don't talk about? (sexuality, death, gender identity, violence, substance abuse?)
2. What are the subjects, whether they have come up yet or not, that you are most uncomfortable with?
3. Are you able to offer an open ear without feeling the need to solve their problem?

Get Your Kids to Tell You Everything Gamechangers

1. For any subjects you find uncomfortable to talk about with your child, ask yourself what it is about that subject that makes you feel uncomfortable. Is it embarrassment, fear, or judgement?
2. Imagine a conversation with your child about one of the subjects on your list. See yourself listening and speaking without judgement. Find a story in your past that you can share to demonstrate how you understand. Practice the kind of nonjudgmental things you could say to keep the conversation going.

Here are some suggestions to help get you started:

"What do you need from me?"

"How can I help you?"

"I get it, I felt the same way when that happened to me."

"I'm not even sure I have ever figured that out myself."

"It's OK to be uncertain."

"I have some thoughts, but I'd rather hear what you're thinking."

"That's an interesting situation. Do you have any ideas?"

Takeaway Tool

"Don't judge. Don't react. Don't solve."

Chapter 11

Is It a Phase, Habit, or Hidden Motive?

"Proud parent of a great kid, who is sometimes an asshole, and that's OK." ~ Anonymous

Being a parent has us navigating through a myriad of phases, habits, and hidden motives from our kids. Those are the trying behavioral weeks or months where we feel like our child needs to be sold to a traveling circus, so we can start over. Even though we are doing our very best, we don't understand, "What is happening!?"

Phases, habits, and hidden motives can overlap to some degree, but understanding the difference between them will help you recognize which one you're dealing with, and what tools you can use to handle it with ease.

Phases

A phase is a change in behavior for presumably no reason. The behavior comes out of nowhere and disappears just as quickly. A phase has a beginning, a middle, and an end. Phases typically last three to six weeks, but can last longer. They tend to have a more brief vibe: biting, hitting, saying "no," coloring/cutting/growing out hair, and not sharing, to name a few. The objective is to spot it and get it to end as quickly as possible.

If you know what to look for, you won't waste terror-filled days, weeks, or months trying to figure out what is going on. In earlier chapters, we talked about big-picture thinking and how it helps us solve problems quickly and not get stuck in the overwhelming micro-moments. By broadening our lens, we can more easily spot trends when they are upon us.

The bad news is: phases occur all throughout childhood and into the teen years...and maybe even beyond...but, the good news is: we can get to the point where we will recognize annoying behavior for the short-term phase that it is. Once you begin recognizing the repetitive signs, you can remind yourself that it is just a phase, and not cause to overreact, panic, or clamp down. You will be able to react with anticipated swift action and not be surprised or angered by the annoying behavior when it shows up.

So many "problems" disappear once we see it for what it is, a short-lived phase, rather than an indication your four-year old will forever be the mean older sibling.

We have all heard about terrible twos. That is one of our first phase tests as a parent. When our firstborn hit age three, my husband and I high-fived ourselves. We downright broke our arms patting ourselves on the back over how we successfully "parented" through the dread that every parent calls the terrible twos. Then, just as our arms were almost healed, all hell broke loose. At roughly three years and two months old, literally overnight, we woke up to our sweet, innocent little boy chomping down hard on our hand and throwing full blown tantrums.

Tantrums were the most unnerving events: toys got thrown aggressively, screaming occurred at the top of his lungs, Tasmanian devil-like energy ran around the room like his hair was on fire and it felt like there would be no end in sight to this new alternate universe.

This went on for about two months. No amount of parenting or grandparenting could stop this freight train. I felt so bull-dozed by his behavior, I actually decided our firstborn might just be no good, maybe a bad seed. My only consolation was being very pregnant with triplets at the time. I had three more chances to get it right! Just as I made that mental shift, he started coming back around and we saw glimpses of his previous sweet self. What a huge relief. It became one of those 'smack your fore-head' moments: oh, THAT'S terrible twos (threes,) it was all just a phase.

By stepping back and understanding this as phase behavior, we won't end up spending a lot of energy 'parenting' it. Wear-ing ourselves out on something that will likely go away on its own will have us making a bigger deal of it than it is. We tend to overreact, thinking we need to parent behavior that is only temporary. This is the time to listen to your instincts and follow your inner voice to slow you down. Most of the time our reac-tion to phases says more about our ego or need to control.

The more we engage, the worse it gets.

That said, you also can't overlook bad behavior. Once you spot the trend, immediate action usually takes care of it quickly.

Handling It:

Handling Tantrums: Don't engage directly. The key with tantrums is to muster every ounce of reserve and be completely unimpressed with the theatrics, having zero reaction. In whatever way possible, remove yourself from the situation - literally and figuratively. The reason you remove yourself is because you can't fight that behavior in the moment. Just quietly get up and walk out of the room. Busy yourself in another room. If possible, even shut a door for a few moments leaving your child to be completely alone while screaming to no one. No audience, no tantrum. Act as if it isn't even happening. Once the behavior calms down, you can say to your child, "I see you are upset, go make yourself happy, you can join us when you are ready."

If handled at home, fewer tantrums occur publicly. A lot of what gets us reacting is our ego. We feel like we have to put a stop to this right now by doing something confrontational. "No kid of mine will be acting like this." It's not about us, it's a phase and means nothing in the overall picture. Handling it quickly at home by quietly and consistently going into another room with the door closed, the phase stops much sooner. There is much less angst on our end, too.

Handling Hitting: I learned this little trick in a parenting class. This might seem contradictory, but it worked after one time. We played the 'hitting game.' Out of the blue one day, your child takes a swipe at you. Being prepared for these outbursts allows us to not react with anger or ego. Once he struck us, our voice got all high-pitched and sing-songy: "Oh, you want to play the hitting game?" We entered into it joyfully and explained that the rules of the game are if he hits us, we get to hit him back. (I am referring to hitting behavior from 2-5-year old's.) We only had to make moderately gentle contact once before he realized he didn't like the hitting game. The next time he tested us with a swipe, all we had to do was say again, "Oh, we are playing the hitting game!" and he would immediately retract his hand and say, "No, I don't like that game." This is about clean, pure consequence.

Handling Biting: This is another phase that comes out of nowhere. Our oldest bit our hand when he was three and our daughter bit her brothers in the playpen around the same age. You might even have a child who bites an unrelated child, but hopefully, if you get the chance to handle this at home, with just family members, it won't affect other kids. Being prepared means you won't overplay this.

Once the bite occurs, do not react with anger. Even though you are fuming, it hurts! Calmly and matter-of-factly remove the child from the scene and explain that mouths have dirty germs and soap will need to be used to clean out the biter's mouth. It won't happen too many times after that, I assure you. All of this needs to be done without anger, just as fact.

At the young ages when phases most occur, kids see things in black and white. This behavior equals this consequence. It doesn't need to be more complicated than that.

Handling Crazy Hair Days (growing/cutting/coloring): While this is a phase, there's also an identity element to it for the child. Allowing kids to experiment with their hair provides us an easy way to give them control over something that doesn't really matter. Letting this go, without judgment or snarky comments is the least dangerous way to give kids autonomy, and it's relatively painless for us. The way we handled this phase was by nodding and waving—we just let it pass. They look back at embarrassing photos soon enough. If your ego is attached to your child's looks, wondering what others will think of *you* when they meet your child with green hair, then it might be more difficult for you to let this one go.

Habits

Habits can be good or bad. For this chapter we will just discuss habits we don't like, for the sake of sharing ways to parent them. Habits are a learned behavior. There are two types of habits: physical (thumb sucking, biting nails, fidgeting, nose picking) and behavioral (lying, blaming others, gaming, back talk.) They all satisfy some root cause.

Habits can soothe stress or anxiety (biting nails,) or they can develop as a distraction (gaming.) However it gets developed, a habit is likely to need our intervention.

The difference between a phase and a habit is that habits have the power to stick around. Habits can become a lifelong matter or a phase can evolve into a habit if it isn't interrupted by us. While habits tend to serve an inner intrinsic purpose, phases are more like harmless mini-tests.

Helping our child change habitual behavior may take repeated intervention followed by periodic disengagement; then possible reengagement at a later time.

Here is a checklist you can run any bad habit through before deciding how you want to handle it:

- ❑ Is there a potential harm in this habit?
- ❑ Is doing nothing a safe option?
- ❑ Can you identify the impulse behind it?
- ❑ What is the root cause?
- ❑ How can you help fulfill the root need in a healthy way?
- ❑ Is it time for professional help?

Handling It

No matter what the result of the intel you've gathered with our checklist, the first rule of handling a habit is to approach it with respect. Only you can decide what habit behavior you are willing to ignore or help your child manage. Habits are serving a purpose, if you try to shut it down, or trivialize it, you'll create more problems than you solve.

Handling Nail Biting: You could try the informative route, explaining that dirt and germs live under nails and show the child that biting nails can lead to getting worms. Try showing them an episode of Monsters Inside Us and this should nip it. However, that's unlikely to work if nail biting is soothing an anxiety or creating comfort, like thumb sucking. As a former nail biter, there is nothing my parents could have done to stop it. The more creative they became in trying to shame me, the more it made me not care as much as they did. Remember, emotional pleas from parents don't work.

If the habit is relatively harmless, let it go. Your child will likely outgrow it when he is ready. In fact, I used that line on my daughter. I said, "You'll outgrow biting your nails when you are ready, like I did." Done. No drama, no shame, no judgement. That is parenting without giving a f^ck.

Disclaimer: I do feel it's important to note here parents should keep a close eye on certain habits if they appear to become Body-Focused Repetitive Behavior Disorders (BFRBs) or OCD, impulse control related. Professional therapy is a great option if more seems to be going on.

Handling Back Talk: First, take this time to re-establish the rules about how you talk with each other. Understand and own any part of the escalation you may have contributed (constant corrections, micromanaging, being bossy.) Make clear you will not tolerate being talked to that way. With calmness and respect, you can both discuss why he feels the need to talk to you that way. Most kids who backtalk are trying to exert independence or don't feel they are being truly heard. This is easy to diffuse with the right tools: restoring respectful communication, owning any of your part, and truly hearing your child. If you are parenting with 'we' in mind and showing respect regularly, backtalk will be minimal.

Handling Blaming: Being in the habit of blaming can become a huge problem. If not curbed at home, blamers enter society and become a pain in the ass as co-workers, friends, or partners. If this habit is allowed to flourish, it turns a person into one whose ego deflects all accountability. A person who blames will also be a person who makes excuses.

To help your child kick the blame game:

Teach ownership. "Mom, you got me to school late!" A blame sentence like that gets the response, "What can YOU do to get yourself up on time?"

Teach mistakes are always okay to admit. "Mom, I broke the vase." "Thank you for admitting that, it's okay, mistakes happen." If a parent's reaction to common mistakes is to get immediately mad or shame the child, it creates feelings of sadness, fear of the truth, or inadequacy. This leads to a child who is afraid to admit a mistake. That's why we want to first check in with ourselves to ask where we might be contributing to their need to blame.

Teach accountability. "Dad, I hate my teacher, she gave me a D on that paper." "Really, you are blaming your teacher for your bad grade?

What do you think you can do differently next time?"

Handling Lying: Kids lie most often when they feel scared, trapped, judged, or need more control in their lives. If our child lies to us, first, we need to consider if we are giving our child a *reason* to lie to us. Remember, if our communication is controlling, pushy, or we aren't doing a good job listening, we can change ourselves to get different outcomes from our kids. We've already talked about not asking direct questions, those are leading questions that invite a lie. We can also gently call them out if it's an obvious bunch of BS. "That sounds odd," or my personal favorite, "I'm confused, how is that possible?" Lying is not something we always have to parent unless it feels like it's turning into a repeated habit, or unless our parenting needs to be tweaked to allow more freedom for the child to not feel the need to lie.

Handling Gaming/Social Media: I've been asked a lot about gaming/social media from parents. Gaming can start as a phase or a habit, but can easily become an addiction. Gaming can start innocently enough as a convenience for parents. Maybe it starts with your toddler gaming on the iPad so he stays quiet. It's helpful to set healthy boundaries, as you do in every other part of your child's life. Teaching kids how to create a healthy balance with their time and activities gets incorporated into their lives long term.

Kids rely on our input. If we get upset that gaming or phones have overtaken our child's time, we need to be reminded that we, ourselves, purchased the games, gaming device, or phone. We have the authority to make final decisions about whether those devices are used responsibly and whether they should stay in the house. If we are for sale on this issue, it does have the potential to become a habit in our child's life, one we or our child will potentially regret later. Don't allow what feels convenient early on to become an issue later. As parents, it's inconvenient to be consistent. While gaming and social media seem to be the biggest concerns for parents as their kids get older, the overall takeaway here is to own our part of purchasing it; whether we originally used these items for distraction or comfort and/or whether clear boundaries were ever put in place. All of it falls on us to monitor, we have the influence to make any and all changes.

Hidden Motives

A child develops hidden motives when their personal *perceptions* don't align with ours. This is typically either on our end, where we might be distracted with work or a new baby, or on the child's end where her understanding of a situation is skewed. Either way, the misalignment needs to be addressed by us.

Dr. Rudolph Dreikurs literally 'wrote the book' (a very dense book I might add) on respectful parenting in 1964 called *Children the Challenge*. Since 1964 many people have offered their version of Dr. Dreikurs' teachings. I'm going to save you from reading 330 pages of a dry 1960's narrative. The huge inspiration from his book, for me, was this sentence: *a misbehaving child is a discouraged child*. Roll that sentence around for a minute.

I don't know about you, but the teenager-in-me who tripped misbehaving kids was fully convinced that badly behaving kids were making the choice to be naughty. I fought the truth in that sentence. You mean "bad" kids just needed encouragement?! The clarity that their behavior mostly comes from their reaction to *us* was hard won for me. Once I bought into it, I saw that sentence is straight truth. Remember, we're taught we are bad parents if we can't change the kid. The truth is, like I've said, to save the kid, we have to change ourselves, not control them.

Turns out, all the years I spent disliking kids was aimed in the wrong direction. It's the parents who should have had my wrath. I see that now that I'm a parent and take ownership for my role in shaping, molding and teaching my kids. Kids will rise to our expectations and leadership. It's also my job to determine why he is discouraged and acting out. Something is out of balance and I can fix it. It's my job to show my child he matters to me and he has an important purpose in our family.

Hidden motives are trickier behaviors to parent because we need to take time to connect with our gut and consult with ourselves to figure out how to change our reactions to affect their behavior. For example, I knew my yelling had to stop and I also needed to stop blaming them for why I was yelling. Self-introspection took some digging deep on my part. But like I said in Part One, all the work I put into myself paid giant dividends with having great kids. While some phases and habits can be overlooked, all hidden motives need to be addressed.

Examples of hidden motives are: a need for constant attention, a need for control/power, and a need for revenge. When a child's motivation is to get any of those perceived needs fulfilled, it's up to us to redirect them to a more purposeful role and adjust our responses.

1) **Need for constant attention:** Some kids create problems just to keep you involved, concerned or to give them attention. When a child is relentlessly saying, "Mommy, watch," "Mommy, let's play," "Mom, Mom, Mom," this is telling you he wants to keep you busy with him. It's not normal for a child to demand that kind of attention from you. So many parents think this is just what kids do, but a child who is in balance does not act that way.

To determine if his behavior is not typical, ask yourself if his action is situation-centered or self-centered? We can step back and determine if his subconscious intentions are to keep us busy with just him or if he truly needs our assistance. Any child demanding constant attention has lost his sense of what his personal value is to the family. He needs a purpose. He incorrectly assumes he needs to be the center of attention to have purpose.

Every child wants to feel like he has value. This attention-seeking behavior might be in the form of whining, being funny, writing on the walls, teasing, or even at bedtime when he finds excuses to keep you focused on him. Any action that keeps you occupied with only him is fulfilling his need for constant attention. We tacitly encourage this self-centered behavior if we don't recognize it as a hidden motive and divert his energy to a more positive role. Instead, find a useful task that only he is in charge of, something specifically suited to him (family photographer, mom's dinner helper) whatever helps redirect and gives him purpose. Schedule one-on-one time with him, go on a 'date' and give him dedicated time with you.

2: Need for control or power: Typically, if the demand for attention does not get resolved, the subsequent hidden motive will become a need for control or power. We've talked about power struggles in earlier chapters. With awareness, power struggles are easy to avoid. If a parent reacts to "bad behavior" by being more controlling, then those threats will be met with a child who doubles down and says things like, "You can't make me," or "No, I'm not going to bed." This is a child drunk with power. We need to recognize that the child's actions are originating from feeling discouraged.

Handling Control/Power: This situation is perfect for giving choices and options to the child. If she is able to choose for herself between parent-approved options, it offsets the need for her to control. Offering choices allows us to withdraw from any conflict. Resist, at all costs, the temptation to punish in this situation. Kids have these hidden motives as a subconscious reaction to growing, learning and becoming independent. They aren't aware they're behaving this way on purpose. That's why the motive is referred to as *hidden.*

3: Need for revenge: Revenge behavior is the graduated response from a child who did not get his attention or control motivations acknowledged. When a child is acting with revenge, get involved immediately. Behaviors tend to be peeing in the closet, hurting others, or damaging property. He may seek revenge as his only way to feel important. He's convinced he's not worthy of being liked and he doesn't perceive that he has any power over the almighty controlling parent. He's acting out with hurt because he sees himself as an unlikable child. This is the most important time to remember a misbehaving child is a discouraged child. In this stage, he feels completely unsuccessful and helpless.

Handling Revenge: A child acting out with revenge thinks he doesn't have worth. A parent might feel like giving up and giving in, but that feeds directly into his view of himself. Don't allow yourself to be convinced that his behavior makes him bad. He needs your encouragement the most now. The temptation is to punish but punishment only serves as proof to him he's bad. Avoid punishing. Make one-on-one time to share his feelings, apologize if needed, and provide tailored activities to his strengths.

Above all, if we take it easy and we are willing to let life be a little imperfect when any of these behaviors occur, we won't treat them with such a serious significance. After all, since kids are adults in training, it's up to us to discern what their actions are *really* telling us and what the best course of action or inaction is from us.

CASE STUDY – Habits

Mom: Jenny. 1 Daughter, 6; 2 Sons, 2

Ever since her twin sons were born 2 years ago, Jenny's daughter Alex became increasingly dependent on her pacifier. Over the past two years, she went from sucking it only at night to continuing into the morning and then throughout the day. Before she came to me, Jenny tried hiding it, telling her to stop, taking away other privileges, and even making Alex stay in her room if she chose to use the pacifier. Nothing worked and in fact the attention on it seemed to make it worse.

When Alex started first grade, Jenny thought her reliance on the pacifier would stop, or at least be relegated to bedtime only, but it wasn't the case. As soon as Alex got home from school she went straight to her pacifier and kept it until leaving for school the next day. The timing of the escalation made the root cause of this habit pretty obvious to me. Interestingly, Jenny had not put together that it started in order to literally pacify herself when her Mom's attention went to the twins after having had Mom all to herself for 4 years.

I talked Jenny through the habit checklist and though she could definitely remember a time when she thought the habit was harmless, she knew for certain she was way past that now. Jenny started panicking, with a list of concerns a mile long, from the obvious anxiety, to concerns about teeth growing in wrong, to problems with socialization, or being seen by other kids and teased. Since Jenny believed the habit could turn harmful, she decided she wanted to intervene. Intervention in this case meant Jenny needed to redirect Alex's attention somewhere else.

I had Jenny sit down with Alex and explain it was time to break the pacifier habit. Alex was given an opportunity to exchange her pacifier for any toy she wanted within the limits Jenny set. The agreement is to 'pay' for the toy with her pacifier. This idea treated Alex with respect. The decision was discussed, Mom set an expectation and Alex could make her own decisions within those parameters. This process was explained and agreed to ahead of time, allowing Jenny and Alex to plan a time for just the two of them to go to the store for Alex to pick her toy. The pacifier got turned over to the cashier in exchange for the toy (with a nod and wink to the cashier, who deftly charged Jenny's card on the sly.)

Even though the event went off without a hitch, the root cause still needed to be addressed in order for the transition of being pacifier-free to be successful. Jenny now sets aside date time each week with just Alex where they spend special quiet time every night before bed. It has been almost 7 months and Alex has not mentioned the pacifier at all.

Phases, Habits, and Hidden Motives Self-Reflections

1. Is your child's troubling behavior situation-centered or self-centered?
2. What digital habits do your kids have? (i.e. Nintendo, Xbox, TV, phone.) Do you have clear boundaries and rules for the use of those devices? If not, why not?
3. Do you and your child share healthy habits? (Physical activity, rest, healthy eating?) What healthy habits would you like to implement?
4. Are there areas in your child's life where she might feel discouraged? Can you see that manifesting in any mis-behaviors?

Phases, Habits, and Hidden Motives Gamechangers

Make a list of your child's most frustrating, concerning or difficult behaviors.

Divide the initial list into 3 lists: #1 Phases, #2 Habits, and #3 Hidden Motives

For every item in list #1 Phases - note the following:

1. What phase is this? Actually give it a title like "The Terrible Twos."
2. Decide on your appropriate response and implement it matter-of-factly.

For every item in list #2 Habits - note the following:

1. Run through the "Habit Checklist" and note your answers:
    a. Is there a potential harm in this habit?
    b. Is doing nothing a safe option?
    c. Can you identify the impulse behind it?
    d. What is the root cause?
    e. How can you help fulfill the root need in a healthy way?
2. Decide what action you choose to take in response to the habit (if any) and what your desired outcome is.
3. Maintain consistency in implementing your chosen response until the desired outcome has been achieved.

For every item in list #3 Hidden Motives - note the following:

1. Is the behavior situation-centered or self-centered?
2. Can you recognize what specific discouragement is manifesting this behavior in your child?
3. Is there something out of balance in the household that could be exacerbating your child's behaviors?
    a. Once you have determined the answers to these questions for the behavior, develop a game plan for how you can help alleviate the discouragement and bring as much balance as possible to your child's environment.

b. Treat that plan as a campaign of support for your child to restore self-confidence and balance to your child's world so that the behavior no longer feels necessary to them.

Takeaway Tool

"Strive for balance."

Chapter 12

Did You Know They're Programmable?

"Tell them what you're going to tell them.
Tell them. Tell them what you told them."
~ Old Sales Proverb (attributed to Aristotle)

When the triplets were babies and Matt was 3 ½, we took them out for breakfast and dinner often. Undoubtedly, complete strangers came up to us and stuffed their faces into the babies' car seats to get a closer look. They'd say, "Are these triplets? Oh, I've never seen triplets before! How cute!" Next came the nunya business questions: was I on fertility, how far along was I when they were born, did any of them need to go into NICU, etc.

This happened with every outing, and each time Matt stood off to the side, feeling left out and wondering why his siblings kept getting all this attention. It made me sad complete strangers had so little situational awareness as to fawn over babies and ignore the three-year-old who was old enough to absorb the feeling of being overlooked.

Soon, I began anticipating this behavior from random people. Once the "stranger danger" commenced, I stood by ready. As soon as they commented on the babies, I'd sweep my hand in Matt's general direction and say, "Yes, and they have the best big brother ever, he helps take such good care of his brothers and sister."

Unknowingly at the time, I was participating in Programming. I watched Matt puff up with pride after his mom publicly acknowledged him and his role as a great big brother. Being one to spot trends quickly, I determined this programming-my-kid-to-be-the-best-big-brother business is incredibly powerful. So much so, I decided to roll it out on a much grander scale. Could their being programmable really be this easy? Turns out, yes, it is!

The transformative power of programming really can't be overstated. We have the ability to prevent our child's temporary setback from becoming a permanent limiting belief. We can help them develop a positive internal narrative that will reinforce their ability to choose how they see themselves and their role in the world.

PS: *First, we must take a silent oath that we will only use this for good and we won't over-use this little secret. When used judiciously, programming is a great parenting tool for redirection. Unfortunately, in the wrong hands it can be damaging. Little children are malleable and impressionable and their parent's opinion is ever so important. Please take care and have deliberate awareness when using programming.*

Reprogramming Nature

Our personality traits originate from both genetics and environmental influences. Some might call this nature versus nurture, but I'm drawing a very intentional distinction here. I'm using the word programming rather than nurture because while nurturing is a continuous process, programming is a more deliberate and precise technique.

When our kids are born and as they develop, we start to notice behaviors or traits that seem to be hardwired within them. They seem to have come into this world with a propensity for certain behaviors. It doesn't matter what our belief is about where they came from, heredity, karma, or divine intervention, the fact still remains that some of these inherent traits or behaviors are positive and some of them need a little... finessing.

The good news is that we don't have to accept these behaviors as just the way they are. By using a programming statement, we are able to easily use our parental clout to change the hardwiring over time.

Here are a few examples for when you spot a trend and it's time to rewrite the program:

Wanderer

For the child who refuses to stay by your side, try telling her that you love what a great listener she is. Ignore the behavior in that moment without direct confrontation, then tell her a bit later, "You are Mommy's best little listener," or "I love how well you are able to listen to Mommy." Soon, she will begin to live up to that statement. She doesn't want to prove Mom's high opinion of her wrong. In the store next time, she will either stay by your side easily or if she doesn't, you can remind her, "Where did my best listener go?" This works well in the moment but it also works at any time. You can make a mental note of the statement and later in the day, out of the blue, program the good listening skill in her.

Stubborn

For the child who will not admit his mistakes out of stubbornness, begin telling him he's open-minded to new ideas and you love how easily he is willing to take input. "Everyone, if you have a new idea about something, run it by Junior first. He loves considering new ideas and being flexible to try new things." Gradually, he will start to identify himself as open to new ideas and taking feedback.

Resists Correction

Along the same lines, with a child who resists self-analysis or accountability, you can tell him, "I love how open you are to learning new things about yourself and to making changes based on feedback. It's so important in life." This one is for an older child who is at the age where he understands how to take ownership for his actions.

Just to be clear, there is a fine line here. This is a technique to be used as a redirect or to get over a hump. Please don't think I'm telling you to spew a bunch of overly positive stuff to your kids for no reason. It's simply a plan of action to use when needed; it's infusing your child with the notion of what they can do, stating it as an affirmation.

Programming Character Traits

With an intentional effort, our deliberate words and phrases can shape our children's character. It's so fun to watch. Programming quickly ignites positive characteristics, qualities, or traits that need reinforcing.

Here are examples using some of my personal favorites:

Instilling Trustworthiness: Make a concerted effort to tell your child you trust her, often. Even if you are questioning trusting her in that moment, tell her you trust her and she will play that sentence in the back of her mind. It's not a 100% guarantee she won't make a bad decision, but knowing you trust her will likely cut in half the amount of times she won't be worth that trust.

"Yes, you can sleep with our puppy, as long as you feed her in the morning and put her out to potty, I trust you to take care of her all by yourself." Yes, this will need monitoring, but it's the belief in her that you are trying to achieve.

"Your curfew is 10 p.m., I trust you to be home on time." Kids are way less likely to disappoint a parent who expresses trust in them than they are to disappoint a parent who lectures and behaves with suspicion.

Instilling Leadership: There will be times we need our kids to step up and put themselves out in front of the pack with a leadership role. It's not always easy for them to highlight themselves in that way, but with our tacit guidance, they will see themselves in that role.

"You show such leadership with your friends, I see how they look up to you." Or, "You are so fiercely protective over your brothers. They are so lucky to have a great sister and leader like you." Or, "What a great captain you are for your team. Your leadership makes sure everyone gets what they need."

In our home this scenario was common. With a messy playroom, I'd ask all four kids to pick it up. Our oldest, Matt, liked to say he didn't do it, the babies did. I'd reply, "Maybe you didn't but I bet Derek, Scott, and Kelly would let you help if you asked them. You're a great leader and role model for them. They do what you do." This acknowledged his point but deftly turned his attention to the needs of the situation and what an honor it is to help and be a leader. He couldn't jump to showing them how to clean and organize fast enough.

Instilling Courage: Sometimes it's hard for kids to have faith in themselves and try something new. With our help, we can make it easier for our child to muster the courage to take a chance on doing something new.

"I love when you help me in the kitchen. I predict you will make a great cook when you get older." Some kids are never allowed to help in the kitchen. Letting kids help gives them courage to cook in the future. If allowed to contribute, they enjoy it and feel pride in accomplishing something new. "It's great how bold you are learning a new sport." "It's fun to watch you have the courage to meet new people so easily." Every word is deliberate, meant to be absorbed into their psyche and stored for future confidence.

Instilling Self-Discipline: We all have trouble getting moving or staying on task. Kids often need a boost while they are growing up. Instilling discipline can be hard to do if our only way of doing it is constant reminding. Try programming, it might take some time but eventually you will see it stick.

The *one time* you see him self-initiate cleaning or exercise or making good food choices, "Boy, I admire your discipline, that's what it takes to succeed."

Making just a few well-intentioned, assuring statements is all it takes to boost your child's self-esteem and turn it into good behavior. It's not often we have such a simple, strategic trick at our disposal to quickly realign how your child perceives himself.

Programmable Self-Reflections

1. Does your child have traits that you have always believed were "just the way she is?"
2. Have you ever used shame or blame to try to "reprogram" any traits in your child? Try turning them into positive statements.

Programmable Gamechangers

1. Make a list of your child's traits that you have always believed were "just the way she is."
   a. Which of those traits limit your child?
   b. Which of those traits positively empower your child?
2. For each item on the list of limiting traits write out the alternative that you would like to instill in your child. Then write the programming statement that you will use to change your child's view.
3. Identify the intended outcome you want for your child. More courageous, or courteous, or trustworthy, or confident, or happy, or ________. Take a moment to visualize that positive outcome for your child. See them in your mind reaping the benefit of your careful programming.

Takeaway Tool:

"I am instilling and reinforcing a positive internal narrative."

Chapter 13

The Wisdom Continuum™: Teaching Great Decision-Making

"Knowledge is knowing what to say. Wisdom is knowing whether or not to say it." ~ Starhawk

I remember being out for breakfast one morning with Scott, one of our triplets, when out of the blue he told me was thinking about changing his lifelong college and career choice. This seemed to be a big departure for him regarding his future. I sensed these new plans came from other influences. At sixteen, it's the age where they really start drinking the teenage Kool-Aid. Friends are their main source of concern and information. His social life came to be everything. He couldn't fully conceptualize his life after the fishbowl of high school.

While I felt confident in the solid framework we built in our kids' abilities to make good decisions, the teenage brain has a mind all its own. This departure in thinking had me slightly concerned, however, because of the weighted importance and urgency in his choice. Time was of the essence for me to make an impact.

I needed to figure out how to get through to him *now,* to help him make a decision for *himself* and *his* future. Not for him to make a decision based on what other people were doing. I wanted to help him back on his own path; but in achieving that goal, I also couldn't minimize his or his friends' ideas.

At that moment, I became inspired to create a visual I now refer to as The Wisdom Continuum. It's a simple, valuable decision-making tool combining all the methods we used over the years to get our kids thinking and deciding for themselves.

Wisdom is the basis from which our best decisions are made. We get our kids to the point of being wise and thinking critically by combining wisdom with what I call 360 Degree Thinking. When wisdom powers 360 Degree Thinking, the foundation for great decision-making is created. And, The Wisdom Continuum can be used to illustrate it.

Wisdom is Teachable

Wisdom is not just information being taught or read, it's the *application* of information, combined with the ability to be predictive when making decisions. To be predictive, our kids need to anticipate the outcomes of their actions. Getting them to the point of predicting the results of their actions, we first want to instill wisdom.

Wisdom is closely linked to common sense. Wise people have certain characteristics that carry them through life with seeming ease. They know how to make the right choices for themselves. And, if it wasn't the right choice, they have the skills and insight to pivot to a *pre-prepared* Plan B.

As kids accumulate their own wisdom, they become more comfortable in ambiguity. Their thoughts and perspectives broaden and they understand situations from a variety of points of view. They understand being wise means they don't need to have all the answers, because they can rely on using observation, past experiences, and critical thinking to make informed decisions. Using these strategies with our kids instills the wisdom they draw from to kickstart their own decision-making process. The earlier we start showing them how, the better.

You may have some contradictory ideas about wisdom and how those who have it, got it. Some feel wisdom is more like a talent you are born with, rather than a skill one can learn, and yet we regularly spout truisms about wisdom coming with age. When we see kids with wisdom, we seem to believe they magically acquired it, and we call them old souls. As parents we're left to feel that our kids are either born with it or they aren't. If we're blessed with a wise kid, it's as if we had nothing to do with it. Or, if our kids seem to be wisdom challenged, it's as if there's nothing we can do about it. To that, I call bullshit. Wisdom and common sense are teachable, trainable and what's more, it's our responsibility as parents to do just that.

360 Degree Thinking™

The process of 360 Degree Thinking trains our child's brain to draw a mental circle around any decision they need to make. The circle symbolizes the various ways they can choose to solve that problem. It's a multidimensional way of thinking that our child can use to analyze their decision choices from every angle. Surrounding a moment with a 360 degree circle gives our child the advantage of considering all available options to figure it out, not just what seems most obvious.

Showing our kids how to think multidimensionally introduces the idea that there is a bigger picture out there. That bigger picture contains information helpful for making decisions. We want to teach our kids the larger meaning to life's experiences while they are living them. Over time, this develops into a self-initiating method for making their best decisions. The sooner we get our kids to create the habit of tapping into their Superpower to choose for themselves, the sooner they will be confidently self-reliant.

The way to teach children to think multi-dimensionally is to begin introducing them to *noticing*. Awareness is a huge factor in incorporating thinking, feeling, and acting into a decision. To help with this, I've broken out the four elements of awareness that comprise 360 degree thinking: hindsight, insight, foresight, and situational awareness. Building moments of awareness into our child's daily lives makes *noticing* become a way of life. In essence, noticing gives them access to their very own *"awareness on demand."*

Hindsight, Insight, Foresight, and Situational Awareness

To teach 360 degree thinking, we must first show our kids *how to* notice and integrate what they learn into their daily routine. Awareness brings to the forefront knowledge they already have access to, but might not take into account. It's right there for the taking, and it's free. They just need to have their attention called to it.

Life is happening all around us. Life, as a source of information, is available to everyone. Our kids will benefit from being aware, at any time, on their own. Over time, they glean what they need and come to trust themselves to make their own great decisions. They don't have to rely on other people's opinions to make a decision, they already have what they need to gain their own wisdom.

Feelings of guilt or being for sale won't cloud their judgment. Their confidence leads them directly to the doorstep of the Magic Mantra; where they are fully comfortable with the notion that they are only in charge of themselves. They won't need anyone else to provide them with the information they can get for themselves, by being aware. Their 360 degree circle can be mapped out and completed independently, using their own astuteness.

Hindsight: Awareness from the past. Hindsight involves applying lessons learned from previous mistakes and successes and taps into one's own personal history for wisdom on what worked and what didn't. Hindsight takes into consideration the results from past experiences to enable making more informed decisions today.

Insight: Awareness from within. Insight is listening to inner senses and paying attention to what feelings tell them. Their body will give them the answers, if they are taught to listen. By connecting to any emotion that creeps in, they can determine if that emotion is tied to, and affecting, their decision. Learning to develop insight, which comes from within, will lead to their most joyful "aha" moments.

Foresight: Awareness of the future; anticipating consequences. Combining hindsight and insight leads to foresight. Foresight brings an ability to predict possible outcomes for any scenario. In the beginning of the chapter, we tied wisdom to the ability to anticipate and have a pre-prepared Plan B. Foresight provides information we need for planning ahead. Foresight can be used to make small predictions along the decision-making process and avoid being caught off guard.

Situational Awareness: Awareness of the moment. Noticing their own actions, as well as other people's actions that are occurring at the same time, enables predicting outcomes based on those actions. Kids can practice noticing surroundings and connecting dots to make critical assessments in that moment. Situational awareness isn't just looking front, back, side, up or down. It's finding the spaces in between, forecasting behaviors and engaging in all senses: being tuned in.

Engaging in focused, prepared thought challenges our child's brain to think on various levels, rather than to only see what's in front of them. By being more prepared, unexpected things happen less often because our kids will be trained in predictive thinking and not just take any situation at face-value.

9 Questions to Generate 360 Degree Thinking Around Any Decision:

1. What is the problem? Define it.
2. What are the different choices you have to solve your problem?
3. What are the consequences for each choice?
4. Who else is affected by your choices?
5. What does your body tell you about each choice?
6. Consider the unexpected option. How does that feel?
7. Is there an emotion tied to the choices?
   If so, can you remove it, then reconsider?
8. Is there a difference between the short-term gain and the long-term outcome?
9. Do you anticipate regret from any option?
   Can you live with that regret?

360 Degree Thinking and Awareness Through the Ages

Cognitive ability and awareness are constantly changing and being developed in kids. Here are some ideas for how to introduce 360 degree thinking during their various ages.

Toddlers: While this age group is a bit limited, there are still ways to help toddlers develop differences in perspective, which is a primer to making their own decisions. Keep it simple and engage their imagination.

Reading Books: Talk them through scenarios from books you read to them. If your book involves going to the park, make comparisons to a time you took them to the park and discuss how the experience was similar or different from the one in the book. Ask for her ideas and observations based on her perceptions.

Picking a Toy: If you are allowing her to pick a toy at the store, prior to seeing all the distractions in the store, ask her to narrow her options down to one or two (puzzles or dress up.) Once she has decided, she gets to go to that aisle only and select which one she wants. If she can't decide between two puzzles or two dress up costumes, you can help her connect with her imagination on how each of the choices will be used. Ask her to consider which of the two she thinks will be most fun.

Kids know the answers, they just need to be asked to stimulate that part of their brain, by asking questions. The key at this age is once decided, they must learn to stand by their decision. No wishy-washy backtracking. Kids are simple at this age and don't grasp nuances yet, so your leadership is important.

Middle Childhood: These are the years to begin giving the notion they have their own control, so confidence builds toward making decisions for themselves. This age group is capable of becoming more logical; reasoning is also kicking in during this time. Middle childhood is a great time to teach observational (internal and external) skills. How to notice, what to notice, and why to notice. Being observant now will lead to the full range of 360 degree abilities later.

Kids this age make observations about friends; who to befriend, who they don't care for and why. If a friend is being mean, they will be able to notice it, but may not have the skillset to do anything about it yet. If your child is trying to decide whether to be friends with someone who acts mean, help them discover all sides of the decision. Was he mean just on that day? Could there be something going on at home? If he's mean every day, do you want to surround yourself with someone who makes you sad or mad? Explore how he can begin investing in other friendships.

Teen Years: Erratic is the best way to describe the teen brain. In Boise, we get foggy days called inversions, sometimes they last for days. The teenage brain is like a foggy inversion that does not lift until the late teens (sometimes later) and only then does clarity begin to emerge. All our efforts eventually start to gel. Life begins making sense for them, they start taking their own initiative to solve problems, and they start grasping the big picture more easily. While we wait for the wires to connect, decision-making and impulse control can be compromised, to say the least. That doesn't mean we can't assist with prompts to help them uncover their wisdom and awareness.

Hopefully by now, your child is able to comfortably learn from his mistakes and he doesn't feel judged for making them. As a teen, he should be able to make a decision and be okay with allowing any consequences to teach him the lesson of that decision.

At this point, guidance from us can be given if asked. When faced with a problem such as which part-time job to take, using 360 degree thinking would mean brainstorming all of his available options and reviewing the pros and cons of each job.

Working at a restaurant keeps him out late, can he still participate in sports, clubs or band? How will that affect homework? A golf course job will kill his weekend, but maybe it pays more. Working in a mall might be fun, what would those hours be and can he balance school, social life, and the job? All facets of each choice are important in making the wisest decision.

With regard to jobs for teens, we found having the expectation they balance school, a sport or club, and a job was a fantastic training ground for decision-making. The kids had to negotiate with bosses to schedule their hours a month in advance. That meant being regularly pissed off because a huge party spontaneously sprung up when they were scheduled to work. We secretly celebrated those moments. The balance needed to juggle such expectations generated life lessons beyond our wildest dreams. It doesn't matter what the expectations are specifically, what matters is that you have them, communicate them and follow through on them.

Fun Awareness Activities

Noticing: Using any public place, practice being situationally aware with your kids. I liked teaching our kids to watch a person's actions over listening to their words. If we were in a restaurant, for example, we practiced assessing the wait list situation. I'd ask the kids, "Does the person taking names seem to have a grasp on the wait list? Does the wait time given seem to match the crowd of people waiting?" Awareness in this case means we aren't waiting around mindlessly assuming others are doing their jobs. If I'm situationally aware, then I'm behaving assertively.

Once seated, we can practice identifying physical characteristics of the waiter (eye color, tattoo, shirt color) and have a contest with who remembers more details. You can also make note of certain features of the restaurant and once you leave, quiz the kids on what they noticed and remembered.

Intuition: This can be played at home or in a restaurant, when you want to keep the kids playfully busy. Request crayons and pick three or four different colors. One person picks a specific color crayon, while the other person's eyes are closed. With eyes closed, the crayon gets placed into his hand and he guesses the color using only his instincts. He has to "feel" the color, "imagine" the color. I even leveled it up by sending "mental messages" of the color, imagining something that represents it. For example, with yellow, I'd focus on mental images of the sun and about 50% of the time it improved their chances of guessing correctly.

The Wisdom Continuum™

The Wisdom Continuum is a simple tool that provides a bird's-eye view for 'seeing' life's phases in the big picture. It illustrates the decision making process and stimulates conversation about how to make a fully informed choice. Using the wisdom continuum, along with 360 degree thinking, our kids become their own devil's advocate.

During that breakfast with Scott, from the beginning of the chapter, I wanted to impress upon him how life is so much more than just the micro-moment he's living in right now, and it's more than the people in the micro-moment. Don't get me wrong, I follow my own advice, knowing full well that I'm only in charge of me, I'm not in charge of him. He knew he had the freedom to make any decision he felt comfortable making. However, we still have to be parents and attempt dialogue with our kids when we see their plans veer rapidly in a different direction. My intention during our breakfast was to generate thought and have him answer his own questions, so he could see for himself the short-sightedness of his hasty decision. Remember, this chapter is about *teaching* great decision-making. Not telling our kids what to do.

At that moment, I urgently wanted to break through the fog of his teenage brain. I challenged myself to come up with a simple, easy way to visually and verbally show him how to make good decisions *for himself*. I was struck by the idea to get out my pen and draw a straight line on a napkin. That line evolved into The Wisdom Continuum and 360 Degree Thinking.

After I drew the straight line, I added various vertical lines intersecting the continuum. The vertical lines represented different points in time; such as phases/events in his life. I explained how he was "here" (first vertical line) right now and in several years, he would be "there" (second vertical line). Then, I instinctively drew a circle around the first vertical line. The circle represented looking at that phase/event from a "full circle" perspective or 360 degrees.

We brainstormed ways to look at his life today and make decisions that project how his life will look when he gets to his future lines.

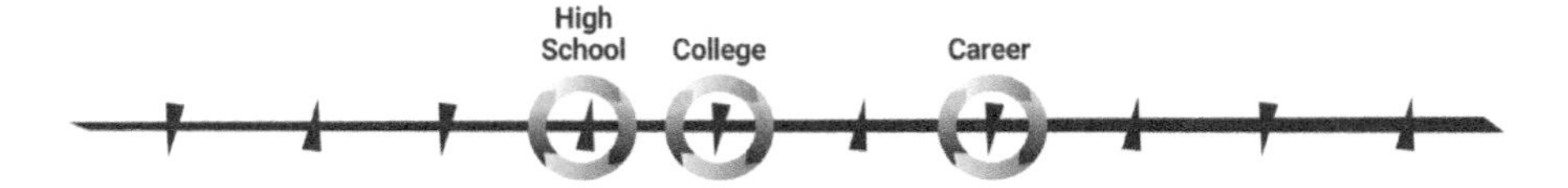

I cupped my hands, mimicking horse blinders straight out in front of my eyes. As I opened my cupped hands wider, I told him his thinking would expand, his exposure would grow and what he found important today would not be what will be important tomorrow. I pointed to the third line and said this is where you will be thriving in your career (programming.) I asked him to connect with himself and base his decisions on what his gut tells him, not what others are doing. My hope was to help him build his own bigger picture. He had to check in with himself to answer all the 360 degree questions for each phase.

This little sketch and twelve-minute conversation made all the difference in his thinking and his ability to see life's broader view. It turned out to be a great partnering moment while we thought out loud, as he answered all his own questions. It became a wonderful opportunity to show him respect as a soon-to-be-adult. This is something we don't always get to do with teenagers.

One of the best aspects to drawing out the continuum is that it doesn't include any control on my part or involve my ego in any way, which can be easily activated when we see a child deviate quickly from their plans. It provides a way to have an honest conversation, where his opinions and feelings could easily unfold.

The light bulb took a few days to fully turn on, but slowly I saw his mind change and soon he started discussing his old plans again. He signed up for a dorm room at his original school choice and began looking for roommates. The best part of all, after enough time passed, he felt as though his changed thoughts were his own idea. And they were, they only needed a little nudge from a loving person who doesn't give a f^ck (wink, wink.)

When we use the Wisdom Continuum, especially with teens, it's important to note that it's useful for either helping solve a specific problem, or it can help us initiate non-confrontational dialogue. Many times, our parental concerns are not seen as a problem to our kids. In the case of my breakfast with Scott, he saw absolutely nothing wrong with the new direction his choices were taking. He didn't find it problematic at that time that he would be discarding his plan to study mechanical engineering as a means of getting into the space program. His lifelong dream could have been cast aside for some high school buddies who hadn't yet formulated their own goals. Never mind that the college where his buddies were going didn't even have a mechanical engineering program.

The Wisdom Continuum is used to spark conversation and get ideas flowing. It's an invaluable catalyst to decision-making, as well as a universal device showing kids how to anticipate the consequences of their life choices and set goals for their future.

8 Questions to Generate Big Picture Thinking

1. What choices can you make today that will set you up for success in your next phase of life?
2. How do you visualize that looking and feeling?
3. Use the continuum to practice 'what if' drills. "If you do this, then what can happen in the future?"
4. Do you think the people you are making a decision for in this moment will have the same level of importance in your life in the future, as they do now?

5. What do you have control over now to set you up for success later?
6. How will this matter to you in 3 months, 3 years, 3 decades?
7. What are the future possible consequences to your choices?
8. How might you feel in a future phase, once you can't go back and change your choice?

Once our kids get the hang of using a wisdom continuum, with 360 degree analysis to problem-solve, it naturally morphs into the more efficient Dynamic Decision Process. They move comfortably between the moment they are in and the bigger picture (where wisdom lives) and then easily make informed decisions for themselves.

Countering Mass Thought with Great Decision-Making

More than ever, we want our kids to feel confident and safe making decisions to stand alone and not succumb to group pressure. Creating their own path might feel harder than it does to sell out, but our kids will have the skills and insight to prevail.

Applying 360 degree critical thought to any problem is the antidote to mass thought. Mass thought has no wisdom, it's just herd mentality. We want our kids to steer clear of crowd-think. Independent thinkers don't follow the masses. They have confidence to access readily available awareness for critical thinking. This is how well-informed decisions are made.

The interpersonal skills learned in Part One of this book applies to your kids, too (no ego, no control, no guilt, not being for sale.) We'd all like to keep our child from following the crowd. By inspiring wisdom and introducing 360 degree thought we make sure our kids aren't susceptible to being controlled and aren't interested in controlling others.

Ideally, we want our kids to not care about being part of the 'in' crowd, and not care about what other people think and do. Looking at a life continuum shows our child all that is ahead in their lives and the problem they are experiencing gets exposed for the temporary moment it is. By looking at the continuum line and thinking big, it's much easier to see this too shall pass.

We are giving our child the ability to also deconstruct other people's behavior in contrast to theirs. They will know, "I'm not less than. What's broken is the crowd. That's something I can fix with a change in my choices and my thoughts."

Using keen awareness, 360 Degree Thinking and The Wisdom Continuum, your child taps into their Superpower and chooses to step out of what feels bad, leading themselves on their own path. They can see their own continuum as well as other people's continuum; "Where is his life headed vs where is my life headed? Today is just a micro-moment compared to what I have happening further down my continuum."

Wise decision making will soon be second nature. There won't be a failure to launch in your household. You will have successfully taught your kids *how* to think, not *what* to think.

CASE STUDY – Wisdom Continuum: Bully Story.

Mom: Nicole. 2 Daughters; 17, 12

When Nicole came in for her first appointment, she was heartsick. Nicole's oldest daughter, Nora, was a senior in high school and had endured substantial bullying since the 9th grade. Nicole felt helpless. She wanted to take the pain away but knew she didn't have control over what happened at school. I reminded Nicole to connect with what she *did* have control over, and that is herself and what she can do to assist her daughter. We drew out her continuum line and marked a vertical line for Nora at that moment in high school, a vertical line for her graduation six months later, and a vertical line for when Nora started college.

Once the lines were plotted, Nicole easily saw the limited time she had left with Nora before leaving for college. We drew a circle around her first line and started 360 degree analysis, "What decisions can Nicole make today to that will ease the hurt from her daughter's bullying now? "What ways could Nicole invest in her daughter immediately to gain valuable access to her so she could share her own experiences and wisdom?" After reflecting, Nicole decided to start a weekly tradition of dinner and movie night, just the two of them. Nora picked the restaurant and the movie. Nicole employed all her listening techniques, they talked openly, with no judgement. This tradition gave mother and daughter a chance to check-in weekly, take a pulse of how that week went and impart some additional feedback, if needed. Nora benefited by having a loving parent help her navigate through the hyper-painful months of mean girl nonsense.

Nicole followed up with me to say this worked fantastically. Using the continuum helped Nicole realize she needed to act fast to come up with ways to ease these painful moments for her daughter, she might not have made that connection without stepping out of the moment and applying the big picture to it. Nicole told me recently she became grateful to those cruel girls, their BS provided her with the impulse to create a fun tradition with her daughter that she might not have done otherwise. Together, they made a lifetime of memories in the process and solved many of the world's problems on those dates!

Wisdom Self-Reflections

1. Are there choices you have made in the past that didn't turn out the way you anticipated?
2. If you applied 360 degree thinking and the wisdom continuum at the time, do you think you'd have chosen differently?
3. Of the four elements of Awareness (Hindsight, Insight, Foresight, and Situational Awareness) which is your strongest?
4. Which elements of Awareness is your child strongest in?
5. What current challenges in your child's life need the Wisdom Continuum?

Wisdom Gamechangers

1. Pick a topic that is a current challenge for your child.
   a. Do your own Wisdom Continuum with 360 degree circles.
   b. Using some of the suggested questions in the chapter, think through your own perspective on their struggle.
   c. Decide what action you can take based on your Wisdom Continuum exercise.
2. Pick a topic or situation that holds a challenge for your child. Make sure it is a struggle they recognize and want to solve.

a. Sit down with them and draw out the Wisdom Continuum.

b. Utilize the questions from earlier in the chapter to inspire you and add your own situationally specific questions to help spur the conversation.

c. Brainstorm with your child, without any agenda, so they can come to effective choices, next steps, and solutions.

Takeaway Tool

"Wisdom and common sense are teachable and it's my responsibility to teach it."

Chapter 14

Punishment Is Pointless

"Patience, what you have when there are too many witnesses." ~ Anonymous

I definitely never saw this coming: me, the poster mom for not punishing kids. Let's not forget, my pre-parent instincts included tripping a misbehaving child who ran around a restaurant. If any parent is going to subscribe to the 'You're going to pay for this' mentality, it's likely to be me. I'm Italian, payback is in my DNA.

But let's also remember, I knew how it felt to be punished, grounded, or have events taken away because of actions or words my parents tried to control or correct. Knowing how punishment left a lingering feeling of frustration and confusion, I knew it wouldn't be an effective way to teach or inspire my kids to give a shit about my rules. I needed new messaging.

If I hadn't been so eager for new solutions, I would have completely disregarded that illuminating nugget, *a misbehaving child is a discouraged child* (Chapter 11, Hidden Motives) as some kind of pansy-ass drivel. But, I had to admit, it made practical sense that we shouldn't need to make our child feel bad in order to make him behave better. There had to be better ways; and there are!

Using punishment as a method to get kids to behave might appear to work on the surface, the first time, but the persisting, accumulated effect becomes resentment. Instead, we want to train ourselves how to turn misbehavior into opportunities for teaching and training.

Kids are Adults in Training

I introduced this mindset in the beginning of the book. But welcome again, to the ultimate centering thought, and really the point of this whole book - ***Kids are adults in training.*** Early in the book, I presented the concept that the answer to raising kids is to take responsibility for your role as the adult, "Change yourself and your child changes." Well, news flash, just as everyt-hing in this book has been training for you to be a better adult in your interactions with yourself and with your child; every single lesson for you in this book applies equally to your children. Because ultimately, ***"Kids are adults in training."***

This is a culminating chapter for two reasons:

1. With the expertise you've discovered from previous chapters, you have the ability to eliminate punishment from your bag of tricks. You see how punishment undermines your other parenting efforts and you know what else you can do to get good behavior.
2. Since kids are adults in training, each and every valuable lesson you have learned also applies to them in their journey toward adulthood. This chapter brings all the book's strategies full circle, culminating in the mind-blowing idea that punishment is pointless.

Making it easier to see how it all weaves together, in this chapter I note each time you can activate some of the concepts you've already learned. This book, like parenting, isn't a straight line, sometimes you'll need to turn around and go back in order to go forward, so I thought I'd give you a hand.

Parenting is complex. If we simply apply broad stroke punishment to bad behavior, our kids will not become accountable and responsible for their actions. We can't be 'remote control' parents, yelling out, "Stop that," from the couch. As convenient as it feels, it won't teach or train anyone. Let's turn what we think to be a punishable moment into an accountability moment. Doing that takes daily connection and effort (Chapter 8.) And, as you've probably already gathered, it sometimes takes intense exhaustive-level effort. But I promise you, it will yield results.

The good news is that if you are this far into the book, you already know how to be a parent who does not punish. Always remember, our kids' challenging behavior is not a crisis for them. It's only a crisis for us. Our reaction makes it a crisis for them… or not (Chapter 10.)

Every time you feel the need to punish, take a breath, repeat *I'm only in charge of me; I'm not in charge of you,* (Chapter 7) and apply the appropriate strategy from your parenting playbook.

Know Your Tripwire

Sometimes punishment has more to do with a tripwire in you than the behavior of your children. Just as your children may have hidden motives (Chapter 11,) the same is true for you. Sometimes we are unaware of what triggers a particular reaction in us to our child's behavior. I call these 'tripwires' because they are often a little thing that can accidentally set off a huge punishment explosion. The more aware you are of what unnerves or upsets you the more you will be able to manage your response.

When a particular thing is overly important to you, it might make your child's 'offense' seem all the more egregious and therefore result in unnecessary punishment.

Be aware of your own personal tripwires and how they affect your position on punishment. Check in with yourself if you find what certain behaviors get to you. We don't need to judge ourselves, just take note with self-awareness.

If you're a neat freak, your tripwire might be clothes being left on the floor. If manners are super important to you and your child doesn't say please or thank you, you may react with anger because your personal tripwire is set to blow if you think your kids aren't using manners.

PS. *If you find you've overreacted and punished your child because of a tripwire, admit to it and own it. Course correction when you are wrong is not weakness, it's having integrity (Chapter 4.) Your kids will learn a hell of a lot more from your admitting a mistake than they will from going through a tripwire induced punishment.*

Create Consequences That Mirror the Real World

Simulating real life scenarios in your home is how your kids learn the inevitable result of their actions. This way of raising kids was earth-shatteringly monumental for me. First, I had to wrap my head around the fact that when my kids misbehaved, it likely wasn't malicious or intended to hurt me (let go of my ego, it's not about me.)

Did they know their behavior was wrong? Absolutely. And that's what pissed me off most, especially being tired and stressed. But when I changed my viewpoint to focus on the centering thought kids are adults in training, I viewed my misbehaving kids as those who needed me to help instill their conscience, their moral compass, and their empathy. I clearly saw the value of real-life consequences over doling out punishment. When utilizing real life consequences, a deeper kind of awareness is created in our kids that demonstrates cause and effect. They understand it's not about doing what we say, it's about doing what's right. They develop a clear sense of what's acceptable behavior and what isn't. It prepares them to make their own decisions based on their assessment of the far-reaching consequences of their actions, rather than judging their behavior on whether or not they can get it past us.

Consequences should always be clearly related to the behavior. They should appear to be a natural or logical result of the behavior. Sometimes it's difficult to figure out how to construct a consequence that is related to the offense. With a little thought and creativity, you will get the hang of it and begin to create your own, in no time. Be patient with yourself in the beginning, it feels a bit unnatural to come up with a related consequence. It's already ingrained in us to dole out old school time-outs and grounding. Those methods may be easier, but we miss the chance to connect, train, and effectively change behavior.

To get you started, below are examples of how to use a consequence that is related to behavior. Applying this thought process will mirror any repercussions our kids will face in the real world.

Naturally Occurring Consequences: These are consequences that occur with no parental involvement needed. It's best for us not to intervene, let them happen naturally and watch how our kids learn from them. At first, this takes some getting used to. Letting the event just happen without trying to fix it, change it, or help feels harsh. Tell yourself this is how they learn; I'm staying out of it. The only reaction we want to have with these consequences is, "Oh, I'm sorry that happened."

Formulating consequences is what led me to create the Magic Mantra. It became easier to have a quick, redirecting thought that reminded me: "I'm only in charge of me; I'm not in charge of you." That's how I taught myself to let go *for real,* and not look back.

Again, this material doesn't come naturally for most of us. Typically, prior to any consequence happening to our child, it's likely you've already made a suggestion or request and your child paid you no mind. You've also probably reminded and made several pleas, all to no avail. This is when consequences (natural or related result) need to take over. For actual results from a natural consequence, let the lesson do all the talking:

Action	Consequence
Don't eat	Get hungry
Forget coat	Get cold
Always show up late to practice	Get kicked off team
Always show up late to job	Get fired
Don't put sunscreen on	Get burned
Be bossy or mean	Lose the friend
Spend all your money	Can't buy anything else
Reaction: "Oh, I'm sorry that happened."	

Related Result Consequences: These are consequences imposed by the parent and should be relevant to the behavior. We may sometimes have these pre-thought out. If not, we will need to take a minute after the behavior to structure the related result so that it is clearly tied to their behavior in a way that teaches the lesson and helps them understand:

> Child rides her bike in the street instead of the sidewalk like you asked; the bike gets taken away until *she's ready* to ride on the sidewalk. Bike riding is a responsibility that is earned. We are building trust by letting her decide when she's ready. It's always our prerogative to reduce bike time if trust continues to be broken. Consequence is bike related.
>
> Child leaves toys all over; toys that are left out get put out of sight and are unavailable until he agrees to pick up the next day's toys after playing. The toy loss continues until he takes accountability that he puts away what he plays with. No yelling, reminding, or bribing needed. Just action on your part,

toys get temporarily taken until he begins to put toys away. No words. When he asks if he can have his toys back, you ask, "Are you ready to put them away after playing?" Chances are quite high he will. If not, it all gets repeated and he goes longer without the toys he didn't put away. Consequence is toy related.

Teen stays out past curfew; curfew time becomes earlier until he earns the later time again. Our personal strategy was to set our kid's curfew to thirty minutes earlier than their friend's. It got them out of parties and events earlier. The kids constantly heard "You won't believe what happened after you left!" As a parent, I love that they missed all the craziest events. If they ever broke curfew, we busted them back to a ridiculously early time. Once they regularly arrived home on time at 9:30, they earned 10:00 and so on. By the time they got their 11:30 back, they were home on the dot or earlier. On the occasion we got pushback for having an earlier curfew than all their friends, we'd remind them, "We have very few rules and don't ask much of you, you have more trust and freedom than most of your friends," (programming.) They always agreed and knew not to push us on our one nonnegotiable rule. No grounding, keys taken, or yelling required. Consequence is curfew related.

Teen sneaks out of house; curfew becomes much earlier. A conversation is had that responsibility is earned, teen must not be "ready" for responsibility if he is sneaking out, therefore, curfew is 9 pm until he's ready to show he is responsible and ready for your trust again. Consequence is curfew and responsibility related.

Examples of the difference between punishing and using a related result consequence:

Brand new puppy in the family, son agrees to feed it but doesn't. He loves playing with the puppy:

SAY: "I'm sorry, but you agreed to feed the puppy and you have forgotten three days in a row. You will have to stop playing with the puppy." He gets puppy play time after he remembers to feed the puppy a couple days in a row.

DON'T SAY: "You forgot to feed the puppy; you don't care about this dog at all. You forget everything, you're grounded. (Sitting in a room being grounded is unrelated to responsibility.)

Siblings are fighting and teasing each other at the dinner table.

SAY: "Boys, calm down and eat dinner or leave the table until you're ready to join us and have manners at the table."

DON'T SAY: "Settle down now or you'll go to bed with no dinner." (Going hungry is unrelated to being rambunctious.)

Your child is a hitter when he gets mad.

SAY: "When you feel yourself getting angry, put your hands in your pocket or clasp them together. Then leave the area and join us again once you've calmed yourself down.

DON'T SAY: "Stop that or you'll lose candy/dessert for a week!" (Dessert is unrelated to hitting.)

Create a Culture of Accountability

Accountability is an enormously important expectation of our kids. Honestly, almost all of what we've covered in this book has involved preparing our kids for accountability, whether directly or indirectly. It's an essential character trait that helps our kids become good leaders, makes them answerable for their words and actions, and helps them establish and achieve goals.

Having accountability ourselves is paramount to nurturing it in our kids. We determine the culture of our household through our rules, our expectations, and even our humor. Once established, it needs to be consistent. When we continually model our standards and have those same expectations of our kids, accountability falls into place much easier. (Chapters 4 and 5.)

Accountability means:

- ❑ Stepping forward.
- ❑ Taking ownership.
- ❑ Admitting mistakes.
- ❑ Doing the right thing in the face of opposition.
- ❑ Being dependable.
- ❑ Having the ability to self-regulate.
- ❑ And…Not Being For Sale. (Chapter 4.)

A person who is accountable:

- ❑ Does not blame others.
- ❑ Does not make excuses.

- ❑ Does not find fault with situations.
- ❑ Does not define themselves as a victim.

When we own our personal stake in our actions and words, we are never victims. We aren't raising them either. (Chapter 3.)

The Accountability Formula: The magic formula for holding a child accountable is to: *Notice, care, provide guidance, give feedback, and see it through.*

Children need to see that someone is watching and paying attention. Kids should know there is a person who is going to act on their misbehavior, consistently. That person is you. You want your kids to refer to you as the parent "who doesn't miss a thing." When parents don't miss anything, it means they are aware of what their child is up to and care enough to call them out. This is done by setting and communicating family guidelines; followed by making sure those guidelines are adhered to. That's when the culture of accountability begins to take shape. (Chapter 4.)

A culture of accountability can only evolve when our child feels safe. A child doesn't feel safe being honest with us if he thinks we will overreact, get angry, or punish him. He will do whatever he can to prevent those reactions and the punishment that he's been trained to expect. As counterintuitive as it may sound, a culture of accountability can only happen when we've let go of control. (Chapter 2.)

Say your child breaks another child's toy. If your usual reaction involves anger or punishment, your kids have no incentive to be honest with you if they broke it. (Chapter 10.) If your child can count on not being yelled at, and knows it's expected they take responsibility and make amends, then it's simply a given. It's a known fact that everyone can rely on. It demonstrates integrity in you and teaches integrity to your kids. (Chapter 4.)

Your child expects that you will drive to her friend's house to apologize for this mistake and offer to fix or replace it. Accidents happen. No need for yelling or blood pressure medication. Situation resolved. Accountability taken.

Quick Ways to Establish Accountability:

1. Set simple, clear rules (reiterating this important takeaway: have very few rules, but enforce the ones you have every time.)
2. Remind kids of their Superpower to choose, standing by their choices brings accountability.
3. See it through, every time. Don't bluff.
4. Say the phrase, "You're responsible for that." (Picking up toys, handing in homework, solving their own problems.)
5. Say the phrase, "I'm sure it was an accident, you can get the rag and wipe it up." (No judgement, punishment, or yelling: just respond to what happened.)
6. Say the phrase, "Go make yourself happy." It's a great way to redirect any negative situation and it puts the responsibility on the child to transition back into a pleasant mood.

Accountability Teaches Responsibility

Teaching our kids to hold themselves accountable at every opportunity helps them shortcut their path to confidence and responsibility. It eliminates their need to get it by trial and error over many years. The earlier we have our kids holding *themselves* accountable the better.

When our oldest was five, he took important items out of other kindergartener's cubbies, as well as some fun classroom props. Now, in his defense, he felt overshadowed by triplet siblings, his dad at war, and me yelling, tired, and stressed. While none of those defenses merited the behavior, acknowledging them as contributing factors was important in getting me to understand his need for attention. Once I took the background factors into consideration, it became clear punishment wouldn't solve his 'bad behavior.' Understanding the nuances leading up to the bad behavior is where genuine parenting occurs.

When I noticed the missing items in his bedroom, I pressed him about how they ended up there. In the back of my mind, I also took note that he must have been feeling pretty bad about himself to have the inclination toward taking other kids' things. I knew I shouldn't treat the symptom (stealing); I needed to treat the problem (need for attention.)

This is where the Dynamic Decision Process 'DDP' (Chapter 5) helped me formulate my response. The situation required my understanding of what contributed to his need for attention and how it connected to stealing. In considering the long-term view, accountability for his actions needed to be established so he knew this behavior is not okay in the future. In considering the short-term view, he needed to personally confront his class to take ownership as soon as possible.

Having a method to use like the DDP prevented me from over-reacting or feeling like I needed to punish him. The Dynamic Decision Process provided me with a structured way to strategize a planned reaction, something else to fall back on that didn't involve punishment.

I could also apply 360 degree thinking and come up with an action plan based on all my available information. The Wisdom Continuum is also an option to show him how his actions might affect his future reputation with these friends. (Chapter 13.) This bit of extra thought and effort to avoid punishing will go a long way toward any child developing coping skills, confidence, and a clear sense of responsibility.

Once I established that he did take those items, we put them all in a baggie and I gently told him he'd be returning them to-morrow, first thing. We role-played how he would stand up in front of his class, admit he took them, and apologize. Then he'd hand each of the items back to his friends. I worked it out ahead of time with his teacher so she could facilitate as much of a hos-pitable audience as possible. He pushed back and didn't want to do it, understandably. He was nervous on the way to school and tried to back out. I reminded him, "This is what responsible people do, we admit when we're wrong, apologize, and fix it."

You can be sure stealing wasn't something he did again. Not because he was punished, but because he learned something. In addition, I took time to give him extra attention at home (which feels contradictory, but was the right answer.) And, I also took him on some one-on-one dates for ice cream or to the park over the next few weeks. This mitigated his 'need' to use bad behavior for more attention. Using the accountability/extra attention combo eliminated any basis for punishment. Punishing him would have served zero purpose. No lesson would've been learned if I grounded him, took away a fun movie night, or cancelled a sleepover with a friend.

Being aware of the bigger picture, fixing what we can (yelling) and explaining what we can't fix (dad at war) will go a long way to keep us and our kids in integrity. Seeing the 360 degree view and taking responsibility for any way the culture of our household has contributed to the situation, while still holding our kids responsible for their behavior leads us to a solution that works for all. That's how true partnership parenting (Chapter 8) and showing respect works. (Chapter 9.)

How the Words "I Trust You" Eliminate Any Need for Punishment

I helped a client, Anna, whose daughter, Jackie, was a junior in high school. Jackie happened to be a highly gifted artist, who was failing art class. She also deliberately missed the bus in the morning and continually busted curfew. Anna, at her wits end, told me, "I took her phone away, took her keys, and grounded her for three weeks." That's when I suspected Jackie must be rebelling from Anna's punishment techniques.

Anna felt out of options, she felt strongly that taking Jackie's keys and keeping her at home was the right thing to do as the parent. But ultimately, she just drove a wedge between herself and her daughter. Remember, kids will react to punishment with what *they* have control over. Whether it's bad grades, getting themselves fired from a job, or ignoring curfew.

What seems illogical to us as parents is really just the kids' way of trying to control *something*, even if it's to their detriment. They don't realize they could be screwing up their future, they are acting out in the only way they know how, to escape parental control and punishment. (Chapter 2.)

I asked Anna, "Would you be open to a radical idea? Go home and give Jackie's phone and keys back. Un-ground her and tell her you trust her. Ask her what she thinks is a reasonable curfew and decide together what it will be. Make that one of the very few rules you have and unwaveringly enforce it. Once there is agreement, Jackie's free to live, learn and be trusted."

After discussing these strategies with her husband, Anna and her husband made the changes that night. They handed back Jackie's keys, removed the restrictive grounding, and both parents told her they trusted her. Jackie reacted suspiciously at first, but her behavior literally did change overnight. Feeling the freedom of her parent's trust, she no longer felt the urge to retaliate against their controlling restrictions.

Anna called me about a week later in shock; thoroughly excited and grateful. Jackie's grades were improving, she started enjoying art class again, and she got up early enough to catch the bus and eat breakfast.

The changes were easy for Anna to make, she just needed them brought to her attention. Why not give something revolutionary a try if you're finding yourself punishing your child repeatedly. The word *repeatedly* is your cue that what you're doing isn't working.

There is no incentive for a child to change a single behavior if he is sitting in his room, miserable. The opportunities to teach, train, and partner are all lost while he sits home 'suffering' for dipping his big toe into testing life's waters.

PS: *Kids love the freedom we give them and the trust we put in them. Losing it is the punishment.*

Pre-Agreed Consequences

I'm going to be brutally honest (there's a shocker!) I can't stand the automatic, habitual use of time-outs. Junior throws a tantrum and mom says, "That's it, time out." Or if he doesn't turn the TV down after being asked a few times and dad says, "I said to turn off the TV, you're in a time out." Those are auto-responses we give when we simply don't know what else to do. If we're truthful with ourselves, we just want the moment to stop. Deep down, we know that a tiny bit of time sitting out *really* doesn't change anything in the long term.

Luckily, there is a variation of time out that works magically. It's the pre-agreed consequence. It works beautifully in conjunction with creating accountability and trust, too. Hopefully you can stomach one last story about our oldest. For what it's worth, he has grown up to be a solid, hard-working, self-sufficient man. He's old enough to give me full confidence that what I'm sharing with you truly does work.

In our makeshift dining room playpen, Matt often asked to hop in and play with the triplets. Inevitably, without fail, not sixty seconds passed before someone cried. After we recognized this pattern a few times in a row, we used the pre-agreed consequence.

The next time he asked to play with the kids, I took him aside and said, "Sure, but if you go in there and someone cries, what should we do about that?" He thought for a bit and said, "I need to come out."

Then I asked, "What should your consequence be if you decide to make someone cry?" He was smart enough to realize I was asking him to come up with his "punishment." He took a minute (he was five) and said, "I'll have to sit on the stairs."

Sure enough, like clockwork, someone starts to cry. The old me would have gotten myself into a tizzy, been frustrated, and yelled, "You always make these kids cry, get out, you're not playing with them anymore!" But the new and improved me, with my pre-agreed approach, reacted calmly and quietly, with no need whatsoever to yell.

ME: "Matt, what did we agree to if the kids cried when you hopped in?" (Note the use of *agreed to* phrasing, it holds him accountable.)

MATT: "I have to get out?" (Note his question tone, smarty pants is trying to see if I'm for sale—I'm not.)

ME: "Yes, get out and sit on the stairs as you said you would. ***When you are ready to play without making someone cry, you may rejoin them.***" (These words are solid gold.) The words give him the power and control he so loved having and wanted.

He's not only doing what he pre-agreed to do, he authored the consequence. I trusted him to sit out until he felt ready to play without making someone cry. After literally twenty seconds he said he felt ready to play again without having anyone cry. I took him at his word and I'll be damned if there were no issues. But, if there had been, I would have repeated the whole sequence. If he continued to test me, he'd lose play privileges for an extended pre-agreed amount of time.

Truthfully, it never got to that point, not even close. (Chapter 4.) Power and control in a five-year old's hands, yet, all while abiding by the rules and administering himself a consequence he conceived. Pretty good shit!

Fear, The Elephant in the Room

Fear is the provocative unmentionable having dominated all of us at some point in our parenting life. Any continual emphasis on what can go wrong means you might have more of a fear perspective than you realize. Being a fearful parent makes you more apt to use fear as a justification for punishment. Fear is also detrimental to your ability to form trusting, respectful relationships, and not just with your kids, either.

If you are using fear as a parenting method, the little voice in your head sounds like this:

- "I'm worried he might…so he can't…"
- "It makes me nervous to think she'll…so I won't let her."
- "I just can't have him doing…so I won't allow..."

If you let yourself parent in fear, you will be over-protective, controlling, and will likely develop an unhealthy attachment to your child. This all comes from a place of being fearful and in the justification you are being a good parent. When your fears are integrated and expressed into your daily decisions, it's crippling to your child. (Chapter 4.) Our fears and emotions burden our kids with anxiety, depression, and insecurities. We don't want our fear generating fearful people.

We all have moments of fear. The trick is not letting that narrative play over and over in our heads to where it consumes us. Whenever I found myself in a fear rut, I put my business hat on and reminded myself of my motto: *"I conquer fear by leading through it; not by succumbing to it."*

In the absence of leadership, fear will grow. The way to get to the other side is directly through the fear. Once through, you will find freedom waiting.

This brings us full circle back to the fundamental truth that: **not giving a f^ck is the opposite of fear.** It's parenting bravely. We don't have fear when we parent without giving a f^ck. If you still have fear, what's your motive? It ties back to guilt, ego, control, and being for sale. Fear is the underpinning of all those. If you feel guilty, work to uncover the fear that lets you feel bad about yourself. If your ego is running the show, find the fear that lets you hide your bare truth. If you need to control, find the fear that lets you not trust others. If you are for sale, find the fear that obstructs your confidence.

Our kids depend on us to have our shit together. They look to us to make unemotional decisions and to trust them with freedom, so they can live their own fearless lives!

PS: *As long as fear has a grip on you, trust can never be present.*

The Other Elephant in The Room

As I was getting ready to finish this chapter, I was asked my thoughts on spanking by another mother. Well, rather than end this book with a deep debate or an admonition, let me simply say this—if you feel the need to spank, take a breath and review chapters 1-13 and then ask yourself, "If my child is an adult in training, would I do that to another adult?" (Chapters 7, 8, and 9.)

Raising kids who don't need to be punished is every parent's dream. That dream is now a reality for you. You are now the stress-free parent who never again has to yell to get through the latest calamity.

Punishment is Pointless Self-Reflections

1. What tripwires are you aware you have?
2. When was the last time you yelled at your child? Was it because of a tripwire?
3. What fears of yours cause you to restrict or punish your child?
4. What's the last punishment you gave your child? What real world consequence could have replaced that punishment?

Punishment is Pointless Gamechangers

Choose one of the strategies below and practice it consistently with your child for thirty days. Note the changes that occur in your child and in you. Is there less yelling, frustration, and power struggle?

1. Focus on pre-agreed consequences with your child in lieu of punishment.
2. Focus on allowing naturally occurring consequences without your intervention.
3. Focus on giving your child related result consequences.
4. Commit to acknowledging, owning, correcting, apologizing when necessary, and eliminating any and all tripwires you encounter or become aware of in yourself.
5. Focus on establishing and maintaining a culture of accountability for your household.

Takeaway Tool

*"Notice, Care, Provide Guidance,
Give Feedback, and See It Through."*

Final Thoughts

The secret is out, by now you realize Parenting Without Giving a F^ck really means we give very much of a f^ck. But what our kids need from us is our involvement, not our over-involvement. Our children need us to help them see their reflection, not our projection. With the *appearance* of not giving a f^ck, our kids grow to respect us, trust us, and become confident and independent-minded. This is the parenting mindset for life. Parenting this way leads us to know when to be concerned and when to let go.

For generations we've been using flawed parenting methods and wondering why we aren't getting results. Isn't that the definition of insanity – continually doing the same thing and expecting different results? Grounding, putting kids in time-outs, and yelling to correct behavior doesn't work. We can't expect behavior changes until we take time to teach our Adults in Training. Shifting our perspective toward respectful, common sense methods will get results that last a lifetime.

If there's only one concept you take from this book, it's that there's no way to change your child's behavior without changing your own first. Changing ourselves is the catalyst to viewing and treating our kids differently. Your new strength and intuitiveness in parenting will directly result in happily behaving, amazing kids.

If you want to connect with all of us who are happily Parenting Without Giving a F^ck, look for **Ask Mom Parenting** on Facebook, Instagram, and Pinterest.

You can also visit www.AskMomParenting.com to discover my latest free download or to sign up for one-on-one mentoring, online courses, or ask me a parenting question via the interactive Ask Mom question/answer box.

I love hearing from parents, send me a note and let me know how Parenting Without Giving a F^ck has been helping you!

**BONUS

What the F^ck is Your Parenting Style?

Take the Ask Mom Quiz and Find Out:

www.AskMomBook.com

Printed in France by Amazon
Brétigny-sur-Orge, FR